GROWING A HEALTHY CHURCH

COMPLETE WITH STUDY GUIDE

DANN SPADER • GARY MAYES

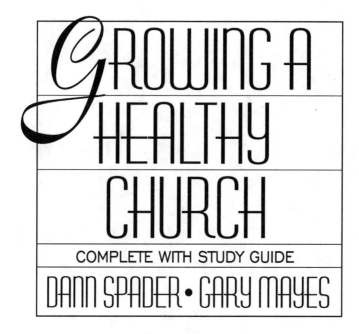

GROWING A HEALTHY CHURCH

COMPLETE WITH STUDY GUIDE

DANN SPADER • GARY MAYES

MOODY PRESS
CHICAGO

5 7 9 10 8 6

Printed in the United States of America

Dedicated to the men and women who have helped shape and stretch the movement known as Sonlife and to the thousands of elders, deacons, pastors, and lay leaders who truly desire to "walk as Jesus did" (1 John 2:6)

CONTENTS

Preface   9

SECTION 1
WHERE ARE WE GOING,
AND WHO DO WE FOLLOW?

1. Our Divine Purpose and Passion   13
2. Our Desired Product   21
3. Christ, Our Example   33

SECTION 2
HOW WILL WE GET THERE?

Phase 1: Building a Foundation
4. An Environment for Growth   47
5. An Atmosphere of Love   55
6. Relational Ministry   67
7. Communicating Christ Clearly   79
8. A Healthy Group Image   87
9. A Prayer Base   99
10. Communicating the Word   107

Phase 2: Equipping the Team
11. The Nature of Ministry Training   123
12. Identifying the Responsive   133
13. Training the Team   141

Phase 3: Winning the Masses
14. Rethinking Evangelism   151
15. Mobilizing for Evangelism   161

Phase 4: Restructuring for Multiplication
16. Leadership Multiplication   169

SECTION 3
PRINCIPLES FOR THE LONG HAUL

17. Cultivating Vision   185
18. The Art of Challenging   197
19. Power to Make It Happen   209

Study Guide   217
Appendix: Sonlife Ministries   270

PREFACE

The typical church is an activity trap. Having lost sight of the higher purposes for which it was originated, it now attempts to make up for this loss by an increased range of activities.

—George Odiorne

We are working harder but enjoying it less. Over the last couple of years several best-selling Christian books have been written on burnout. Activities, options, and distractions abound in our churches.

Jesus' disciples were filled with joy as they ministered, and the early church came together with "glad and sincere hearts . . . And the Lord added to their number daily those who were being saved" (Acts 2:46-47).

Although many churches in America are growing, most are not. And the growth that is occurring is all too often a mere "shuffling of the saints" rather than true conversion growth. The average church in America is seeing less than a 3 percent conversion growth rate. To be healthy, church growth experts say we need to be seeing 10 percent growth a year.

Where have we gone wrong?

More than fifteen years ago, the seeds for this book were planted when a professor challenged Dann to look closer at the methods of Christ's ministry. That study lasted more than ten years—and ended with the conclusion that Christ gave us not only a message of reconciliation but also the method. As Robert Coleman said, "the Master disclosed God's strategy of world conquest." When you examine His plan, you will "be amazed at its simplicity and wonder how [we] could have ever failed to see it before . . . the basic philosophy is so different from that of the modern church that its implications are nothing less than revolutionary" (Robert Coleman, *The Master Plan of Evangelism* [Old Tappan, N.J.: Revell, 1964], p. 18).

This book is an attempt to communicate our understanding of that revolutionary strategy. Through the work of Sonlife Ministries over the last ten years, we have met thousands of elders, pastors, lay leaders, and students across North America who desire to "walk as Jesus did" (1 John 2:6). We believe that the ministry of obedience to the Lord in fulfilling the Great Commission is simple, not complicated.

We have sought to write this book in an easy-to-read format. Our desire is to give you a fresh look at how Christ developed His ministry. Paul wrote to the Corinthians and warned them not to "be led astray from your sincere and pure devotion to Christ" (1 Cor. 11:3). It is our desire that this book would bring us back to our "higher purposes" of seeing the Great Commission fulfilled within our own lives and the life of our local church.

SECTION 1

WHERE ARE WE GOING,
AND WHO DO WE FOLLOW?

...PASTOR BOB BREAKS THE BAD
NEWS TO HIS WIFE AFTER
EXAMINING ANNUAL STATISTICS...

"HONEY... I SHRUNK THE CHURCH!"

1

OUR DIVINE PURPOSE
AND PASSION

A story has circulated about his last season as head coach of the Green Bay Packers. Certainly those who worked for and around him knew the game of football. But on this day, Vince Lombardi faced a difficult challenge: where to begin after yesterday's humiliating defeat. There was little he could say to his team that hadn't already been said. There were few aspects of the game that they had not practiced and analyzed extensively. The men were professionals. They knew that their performance on the field yesterday had been atrocious. They knew their performance bore no resemblance to their game plan. They were angry, frustrated, and disappointed, to say the least.

In his remarkable manner Lombardi met the challenge head-on. Picking up the familiar oblong, leather ball, he went directly to the heart of the matter. In a deliberate manner he brought everyone's attention back to the basics with five simple words: "Men, this is a football." One of his players who understood exactly how badly they needed to review the essentials spoke up, "Hold on, Coach, you're going too fast!"

The challenge before us is similar to that of Lombardi's. In the church today there are few matters we haven't studied and discussed extensively. There is little to be said that will not sound familiar. And yet there is much room for us to grow in our effectiveness at carrying on the ministry of Christ.

Just as Lombardi began that day by forcing his men to look at the fundamentals of the game, we begin by examining the purpose that lies at the heart of everything we do. We begin by lifting up our "football"—our purpose—and reviewing exactly why we are here.

BACK IN THE BEGINNING

Imagine what the early followers of Christ experienced at His ascension. Surely there was exhilaration at the moment Jesus was carried up into heaven. But just as surely some profound questions must have been rumbling through the crowd in the moments afterward. "Now what?" "What are we supposed to do?" "Where are we supposed to do it?" "How do we begin?" "How should we continue, now that Jesus is gone for good?"

Have you ever wondered about the things the believers must have discussed together while they waited for the promised Holy Spirit? In Scripture we get the distinct impression that they spent the days before Pentecost waiting, meeting, and praying together. Surely they spent much time discussing how Christ intended them to carry on His work.

Put yourself in their shoes. You have no church growth consultants to call on for wisdom. There are no other churches to whom you might go for assistance. You do not have a single book to which you can refer. The New Testament does not yet exist. You don't even have the latest gospel tract to help you share the gospel. Where can you turn for answers to the momentous questions of direction and purpose you face as an infant church?

THE COMMAND OF CHRIST

Sometime shortly before the ascension Matthew tells us that Jesus gathered the eleven together for a time of instruction. Perhaps it was a final training and review session. In that setting He clearly communicated the mission to which they—

and we—are called. If we listen with their ears and look with their eyes, we may gain fresh insight into verses that can otherwise be obscured by their familiarity. Become one of the eleven disciples in this intimate setting. Feel the wind against your cheek and the grass under your feet as you listen to Christ communicate the passion of His heart.

Your journey together to the rendezvous was filled with speculation about Jesus' plans. Something was up. All eleven of you had sensed it from the moment He asked you to meet Him in the hills. Over and over again while you walked you asked, "Is He about to leave us—again?" Concern over the possibility that Jesus might be leaving for good punctuated your journey with periods of long awkward silence.

Jesus was waiting for you when you all arrived. It felt good to be with Him as it always did. But from the first moment it was apparent that He had something specific on His mind. He obviously wanted this meeting and the words He would say to make an indelible mark. "All authority in heaven and on earth has been given to me. Therefore go and make disciples of all nations, baptizing them in the name of the Father and of the Son and of the Holy Spirit, and teaching them to obey everything I have commanded you" (Matt. 28:18-20).

His words hit home loud and clear. In His message was a single profound command, "Make disciples." You knew what that meant because you were a disciple. The others who had been faithfully following Jesus were also called disciples. His plan was that you would help others follow Him just as you had followed Him. Jesus had summarized His passion and His design for the ministry that you were to continue. It was to be identical to the passion and plan of His own ministry. Everything was clear. You and the other disciples now understood what to do—make disciples and help others become followers of Jesus like you.

Perhaps the most encouraging and reassuring aspect of Jesus' instruction was that you already knew how to win and build disciples. Not only had Jesus described what to do, but during the course of His life He had demonstrated how to do it. For more than three years you had watched Jesus make disciples, and now He was sending you out to continue that very thing.

The task before the leaders of His church today is really no different than it was for those who formed that initial cadre of believers. *We are called to restore to the local church a passion for obeying the Great Commission.*

OUR DISCIPLESHIP DILEMMA

Wait one minute! Haven't we always discussed discipleship as an optional, though desirable, aspect of ministry? Isn't it a little extreme to elevate disciple making to center stage?

Perhaps you are uncomfortable calling disciple making the purpose of the church. Most churches are apt to refer to discipling as *one* of the things they do as a church, not the *central* thing. One reason for this dilemma is the myriad ways we use the term: "disciple," "discipling," "discipleship."

In one instance we speak of discipleship as a special elective taught for the "really committed" in a Sunday school class. In another we say it is a one-on-one relationship between a mature believer and a young Christian. We package "discipleship programs" as intensive curricula designed to provide doctrinal and practical foundations for believers. We have ministers of discipleship, discipling workshops, and scores of books that address the subject.

Yet we are rarely comfortable using the term "disciple" to describe ourselves. In fact, Christians seem to have adopted a multitiered view of spirituality. On level one are new Christians, who are young in their faith. "Regular" Christians comprise the second and largest level. And the highest level is reserved for disciples. In this view disciples are superspiritual people who go above and beyond the call of duty in their pursuit of Christ. *A disciple is certainly more spiritual and more aggressive about his faith than I am,* we think.

This confusion with terms is more than a semantic problem. It is true that we have confused our definition, but the real problem is that, in one way or another, our experiences have altered our understanding of what Jesus meant in His Great Commission.

THE HEARTBEAT OF HIS COMMAND

What exactly did Christ command in this ministry agenda? Perhaps in the past you have heard or given messages emphasizing one of four distinct aspects of this command: *going, making disciples, baptizing,* or *teaching.* All are important. All are fundamental aspects of ministry. But what is the main point?

The reality is that in these verses there is only one command. And it is emphatic in the original: "Make disciples!" The other instructions are participles that tell us where and how to carry out that command. Jesus intends the driving passion of His church to be Great Commission oriented discipling.

The Great Commission, contrary to many people's thinking, is not just a missions emphasis, nor is it just a focus upon evangelism. It is the mandate of making disciples—a balance of winning people to Christ, building them in their faith, and then equipping them to share in the further work of the Great Commission. *The Great Commission is the primary work of the church!*

What about the idea that the church exists to glorify God? No argument. Obviously we can say that the church exists to glorify God. But the real question is how do we do that?

In John 17 Jesus gives us the answer in His intimate conversation with His Father. "I have brought you glory on earth by *completing the work* you gave me to do" (v. 4, italics added). What was that work?

It wasn't just His death, as He was yet to die for our sins. It was the work of His life—a life of making disciples who would carry the message and method of reconciliation around the world. The whole context of His prayer in John 17 focuses on the work He had done among His disciples and the work that lay ahead for them. That is why Jesus said, "As you sent me into the world, I have sent them into the world" (John 17:18).

Jesus glorified His Father by making disciples, and the church will glorify God by doing the same. His final words on this planet reiterated the message of His life: "Go and make disciples of all nations, baptizing them in the name of the Father and of the Son and of the Holy Spirit, and teaching them to obey everything I have commanded you" (Matt. 28:19-20).

The biblical concept of discipling is not nearly as difficult as we have made it. The solution is to understand what Jesus meant when He used the term *disciple*. You see, when the eleven disciples heard Jesus speak those final words, they immediately knew what He meant by "disciples."

A disciple is literally a follower, a pupil, a learner, an apprentice. He is one who has decided not only to follow his master but also to become like him. In the book of Acts the term was used to denote members of the new religious community, so it was almost synonymous with the term "Christian."[1] It is not a mystical superspiritual quality but simply describes a person who follows Christ and intends to become like his Master.

When you catch a glimpse of discipling from this perspective, you realize it must mean helping people follow Christ from wherever they are spiritually. If a person is apart from Christ completely, it means attempting to help him become a follower of Him. If someone already knows Christ as his Savior, discipling means helping him follow Him more completely and consistently. Therefore, a true discipling ministry will include every aspect of *winning* people to the Savior, *building* them up in their faith, and *equipping* them to win and build others.

The phrases that surround the command to make disciples in the Great Commission reinforce this broad agenda. Remember the three participles found in Matthew 28? "Going" tells us to be aggressive in winning people for Christ. "Baptizing" makes clear that our agenda for new believers is to identify them with the Savior, building them in their faith. And, "teaching them to obey" instructs us to explain to believers all that is necessary to walk in active obedience to the Savior. This teaching should "equip" people to make a difference for Him in the lives of others, walking as Jesus did (1 John 2:6). On every front, the disciple-making process described in the Great Commission is bold and aggressive.

It is time to allow God to challenge not only our understanding of disciple making but the very agenda of our ministries. "Far too many churches are active in teaching but passive in evangelism. The church needs to rethink its vision. Not only individuals, but entire churches should become involved in the Great Commission."[2]

If we understand that by His use of the term *disciple* Jesus was referring to every man or woman who would belong to Him and would seek to become like Him, and if we realize that making disciples is the purpose that should be at the heart of everything we do, then Great Commission discipling could be defined this way: *Doing everything possible to help every person possible pursue Christ more completely and consistently.*

TRANSLATING PURPOSE INTO AN AGENDA

Purpose is important. It keeps our attention focused on what we are supposed to do. Vince Lombardi understood that.

Purpose can keep us from being distracted by myriads of possible programming ideas. On a pragmatic level it helps determine our agenda. We ask ourselves, What should we do in order to best accomplish our purpose?

To clearly understand the purpose and passion Christ gives His church is a challenge to every person in ministry leadership. Our challenge is to build ministries that effectively meet people wherever they are spiritually and help them grow in their relationship with Christ. This challenge is not easy. It is much easier to go along with the flow, but choosing the path of least resistance is not one of our options.

One more thing, clear purpose and risk are close companions. When your purpose is crystal clear, there are times you will discover the need to alter your course. A consuming purpose may call for new endeavors, experiments, and journeys into uncharted waters in order to be fully achieved. Risk accompanies new endeavors because any kind of change, no matter how slight, takes people into the unknown. Of course risk is not easy. Yet a firm grasp on purpose and the direct relationship of change to that purpose enables people to be more willing to take needed risks.

On the positive side, clear purpose not only enables people to risk, but it fuels faith at the same time. When we move ahead with the absolute confidence that what we are pursuing is the expressed purpose God has for us, we can move ahead in faith. We can make decisions anticipating the powerful work of God to accomplish His purpose because our agenda has aligned itself with His desire.

Risk a little now, asking yourself hard questions about your ministry. How clearly committed is your ministry to Great Commission discipling? Perhaps you are firmly committed to this purpose that Christ laid out for us, but how well do your coworkers in ministry share your commitment? How accurately do the people who share the leadership in your church understand what God has called you to? What might be done in the near future to communicate God's purpose for His church with the people of your church?

Hold up the football, and look at it in a fresh, new way!

Notes

1. Walter Bauer, *A Greek-English Lexicon of the New Testament and Other Early Christian Literature,* translated and adapted by William F. Arndt and F. Wilbur Gingrich, 2d ed. (Chicago: U. of Chicago, 1979), p. 486.
2. Aubrey Malphurs, "Why Are Fewer and Fewer People Going to Church Today and What Can We Do About It?" *Kindred Spirit,* Spring 1990, p. 7.

2

OUR DESIRED PRODUCT

Imagine that you were given the job of running a shoe factory.
By what standards would the success of your factory be measured? It would not be the busyness of its employees, nor the
appearance of its building, nor the size of its structure; your
success would be determined by the quality of the shoes you
produced. The task of a shoe factory is to make shoes.

In chapter 1 we explored the product that the church is to
be producing—disciples. Are we producing them? Are we winning, building, and equipping believers?

> Forty years ago two out of every three Canadians attended
> church on any given Sunday. Four years ago it was one out of
> every three. And in June [1990] a Gallup poll reported a record
> low: one out of every four Canadians attended church. From
> two-out-of-three to one-out-of-four in forty years is a fast slide.
> It's impossible to explain it away.[1]

> Most Christians are not aware that the church in America is in
> numerical decline. In fact I now refer to it as "the shrinking
> American church." . . . Dr. Win Arn reports that 80 to 85 per-
> cent of the churches in America have either "plateaued" or are
> dying. While the typical church in America is declining, the un-
> churched population is growing. Dr. George Gallup conducted a
> survey in 1978 and discovered that 41 percent of America was
> unchurched. He conducted the same survey in 1988 and the fig-
> ure had climbed to 44 percent.[2]

> If top priority is not given to evangelism by our churches, in two generations the church in America will look much like its counterpart in Europe.[3]

> At a recent "missionary conference" of Muslim leaders in Los Angeles, they set as their goal the winning of 50 to 75 million Americans to the Islamic faith. This they deemed as a reasonable goal citing historic precedents of conquest in North Africa, Egypt, and Indonesia.[4]

The church of Christ is commissioned with a task that is nothing less than incredible. This task is simultaneously global in its scope and yet intensely individual in its focus. The humbling yet motivating truth is that God has chosen to carry out the eternal work of His kingdom through His church—through our own churches. To progress in this work requires that we translate our purpose into a plan of action.

What does a ministry with a passion to carry out the Great Commission look like? What kinds of programs and plans are needed to meet the needs of a variety of people at different levels of spiritual interest or maturity? Answering questions such as these will keep us focused on the strategic importance of the methods, or programs, of ministry.

You see, our programs—the way we structure our people relationships—will determine how well we are able to carry out the Great Commission. We can hope for non-Christians to be reached. We can pray for disciples to be developed. We can wish for believers to be mobilized. But for those goals to become reality we must develop delivery systems that will facilitate them. The delivery systems are generally our programs—systematically planned methods for ministering to people where they are.

PRINCIPLES TO GUIDE OUR PROGRAMMING

Programs in the church are a funny thing. Everyone would agree that we have programs to help us carry out our God-given purpose. Yet, at the same time, they have the ability to take on a life of their own. "Sacred cows" we call them. For whatever reason, programs often begin to exist for their own sake. Their originally clear purpose becomes mired in an unclear swamp of busyness and activity. Leaders become consumed with "getting ready for Wednesday night." At some point no one remembers how a program got started, and everyone settles for the philosophy that as it was in the beginning, so shall it ever be.

Do not be deceived; programs are not neutral elements in our ministry. They are the means by which we structure ourselves to accomplish the work God has called us to. They are the vehicles that carry us toward our goal of Great Commission disciple making. We must learn to let the programs of our ministry serve as tools to help us, not as taskmasters that control us. Therefore, it is absolutely critical that we come to grips with three fundamental principles that should guide our programs.

1. Our effectiveness in winning, building, and sending disciples will be either enhanced or hindered by our programming structure.

There is probably not a single church or ministry that does not explicitly state its intention to reach the lost. Yet many churches have become so busy with activities for believers that they have little time, energy, or tangible resources left to reach out to the lost. Other churches clearly affirm their desire to disciple believers but have no program especially designed to fulfill that goal. (Understand that the purpose of these comments is not to point an accusing finger at anyone's church or ministry but rather to get you to think about how your programming contributes to your ability to accomplish what God has called you to do.)

The program structure of our ministry will either enhance or hinder our ability to carry out our purpose. Unfortunately, because programs tend to expand in scope and proliferate in number, they often get a bad rap. Programs are not evil. Rather, they are a structured means of bringing people together to fulfill our divine purpose. They are a means of structuring relationships so that the discipling process can take place intentionally.

Suppose we look at a typical evangelical church to examine the impact of their programming on their ability to reach people. Depending on their size, they would probably carry programs like the following.

On Sunday:
- Sunday school for all ages
- Morning worship services
- Children's church
- Evening service
- Children's choir or other creative program during the evening service
- Periodic all-church fellowship events
- Youth group "fellowship" or other get-together

During the Week:
- Small group Bible studies
- Wednesday night programs: choir practice, children's club, youth group Bible study, prayer meeting
- Evangelism training
- Committee meetings and board meetings
- Sports teams

Does that sound familiar? Those are all fine programs, but think about the people for whom they are designed. Let's sit down with the pastor, and ask him to explain the primary purpose of each program.

"All right, let me see now," he says, beginning to think about each program.

"Sunday school—that sort of speaks for itself. It is designed to teach the Bible to our children and adults. The purpose is clearly to help them grow.

"Worship service—this also is clear. It is the focal point of the week as the body gathers to worship and be fed. Sometimes we give an invitation in case non-Christians are in attendance, but our purpose really is to help people worship and grow in the Lord."

"What about Sunday evening's service?" we ask.

"Sunday evening is much more informal. This is when our really committed people attend, so we sing a bit more, sometimes do some sharing, and the preaching is designed to help them become more grounded in the Lord. Our children's program is intended to give our Christian children a chance to express their faith in song.

"The purpose of our small group Bible studies is to help the person who wants to grow in his or her faith and knowledge of the Word. These studies offer encouragement for people as they live and work in the world. They also provide a place of belonging and fellowship.

"Wednesday night is 'family night,' where we offer something for each member of the family. The Christian families in our church arrive together and then participate in the program of their choice.

"Evangelism training on Thursday night is a training ground for people who want to learn to share their faith in an articulate and confident manner. They follow up on people who visit our church and seek to share the gospel with them. Often the people we visit are Christians already, but the visitation process is still very encouraging to our people."

As you can see, although the church calendar is full, almost every activity is designed to serve those who are already Christians. What is being done to reach those who are lost? What is being done to minister to those who are *not* yet anxious to grow in their faith? Just as important, what specific things are being done for the believer who has grown substantially and now really wants more?

Your church may or may not be like this example. However, evangelical churches do commonly share this predicament. Frequently 80-90 percent of a church's efforts are geared for the growing Christian, and little or no corporate efforts are focused on other levels of spiritual need. When time, energy, and people are spent on growth-oriented activities, not much is left over for other priorities of ministry.

Could that explain the plateauing or declining attendance of so many churches as referred to at the beginning of this chapter? Do we need to rethink and retool our program structure? Do not be fooled. Our effectiveness in winning, building, and sending disciples will either be enhanced or hindered by our programming structure.

2. The goal of our programs is to develop a well-balanced ministry—the kind that can minister to people at various levels of spiritual maturity and interest.

Without stereotyping or pigeonholing anyone, how would you describe people in your community spiritually? Have you ever wrestled with that thought? If our aim is to reach people at their point of need and help them follow Christ, then we need to gain a better understanding of where they are now.

If we don't do that, we become susceptible to two damaging traps, both of which can hinder the scope and effectiveness of our ministry. The first trap is focusing all of our attention on those who already attend our church. That assumes the people of our church will carry out the work of evangelism on their own with little need for assistance or encouragement. The second trap is assuming that if someone's needs aren't being met, it is probably his or her own fault. This is exhibited in comments such as, "Her problem is that she's just not committed enough." Or, "If he would do more than only attend the Sunday morning service, maybe he would find the kind of help he needs."

A discipling ministry that is committed to fulfilling the Great Commission must come to grips with people's spiritual status and then develop a ministry that can minister to them. Here is a general list of six kinds of people in your community and church who need to be primary targets of your ministry.

The secular, or lost, person. This is the person who has little or no knowledge of God and very little interest in correcting that situation. He does not attend church unless he is obligated to attend a church wedding or funeral. He does not listen to religious radio or TV unless he accidentally turns to the wrong station, in which case he listens only long enough to recharge his defenses. Jesus consistently took His message to these people. Look afresh at His encounters with the Samaritan woman, the tax collector, and so on.

The disinterested, fringe attender. We tend to be more familiar with this person and his needs than we are the totally secular person. This person may be a double-dipper—one who does his religious duty on the prescribed semiannual holidays, Christmas and Easter. Perhaps he is the spouse of a believer and attends church services periodically to keep peace at home. He has some limited contact with the church and therefore with the gospel, but he has not made a personal commitment to Christ. In Jesus' ministry these would be the people drawn to Him because of His miracles and healings. This person got on the band wagon because of the external excitement of it all.

The curious seeker. This is the person who has moved from one of the first two categories to a position of interest. In some cases he has seen something different in the life of a friend. In other cases God has broken through to him via a traumatic event or the strong internal working of His Spirit. For whatever reason, he feels internally compelled "to give God a chance." He is looking to see if God really does have something to say after all. He is curious, wanting to check things out, to look a little closer. Zaccheus would likely fit into this category.

The growing Christian. By the time an individual is in this stage, new birth has taken place. He has been convinced. He has become a follower of Christ and is growing in that relationship. He wants help in his pursuit of Christ. He needs to be "rooted . . . and established in [his] faith" (Col. 2:7, NASB*).

* *New American Standard Bible.*

The serving Christian. This is the backbone-of-the-church believer. He is not only growing spiritually but serving others as well. He wants to be equipped so that he might be more effective in serving Christ and his church and in reaching out to the lost. This is the worker whom Jesus challenged us to earnestly pray for.

The leader/shepherd. A believer who is not only growing and serving but shepherding a segment of the ministry is a leader. As a shepherd he is working to guard, guide, and nurture the segment of the flock entrusted to his care. He is eager to learn how to multiply the ministry by equipping others. This person often needs to be challenged as well as trained for ministry. In Jesus' ministry the twelve were being nurtured and equipped for this level of ministry. In fact, approximately two and a half years into His public ministry you can see Jesus delegating greater and greater ministry responsibility to the twelve.

Is this beginning to sound complex and unmanageable? Fear not! It is possible to meet the needs of all these different people with four types of programming. By carefully planning four types of regular programs, you will develop a ministry that can meet people wherever they are.

Outreach programming is designed to expose non-Christians to Jesus Christ. The goal is to see them either accept Christ or move closer to accepting Him. Practiced churchwide, this encourages and assists believers to reach others.

Growth programming helps Christians to follow Christ more completely and consistently.

Ministry training programming equips workers to share in the work of the ministry.

Leadership training programming is designed to equip those who are ready to shepherd a segment of the flock so that they might multiply themselves and multiply the impact of the ministry.

If we are going to be committed to fulfilling the Great Commission, it is essential that we develop ministries that meet people where they are. Carrying out the Great Commission

PURPOSEFUL PROGRAMMING

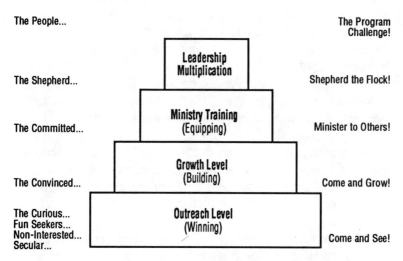

The People...   The Program Challenge!

Leadership Multiplication

The Shepherd...   Shepherd the Flock!

Ministry Training (Equipping)

The Committed...   Minister to Others!

Growth Level (Building)

The Convinced...   Come and Grow!

Outreach Level (Winning)

The Curious...
Fun Seekers...
Non-Interested...   Come and See!
Secular...

A "Great Commission" ministry is one that has a balance of winning, building, and equipping—ministering to individuals at their level of interest.

locally means going after people at all levels of spiritual interest. Those four kinds of programs can create an environment to do that.

It is critical at this point to understand that we must have a balance of winning, building, and equipping activities. Only then will we truly be able to "mature" disciples as Jesus did and as He commanded us to do. If all of our programming—or the vast majority of it—focuses on nurturing believers, their growth will actually be stifled. All intake and no output cannot help but cause stagnation. Only as we give away our faith do we gain the fullness of our faith (Philem. 6). Only as we live out our faith are we truly fulfilling Jesus' command for His church.

Throughout the following chapters we will examine each area of programming in more depth. We will also take a closer look at the life of Christ to see how He implemented each of the four kinds of ministry. But before moving on, there is one more principle of programming to explore.

3. Doing a few things well is more effective than doing many things in mediocrity.

You have seen this principle at work in your own backyard. If you take a large quantity of water and pour it out, it quickly spreads out over the ground. If you take the same amount of water and run it through a large pipe, you can channel it for better control. However, if you force that water to travel through a half-inch garden hose with a nozzle you instantly have a much greater impact because of the increased water pressure. What makes the difference? The narrow focus of the hose prevents indiscriminate dissipation. "If providing diversity undermines the quality of output, the best bet would be to provide fewer options, but higher standards."[5]

Undoubtedly, you have been in situations where you had too many things going on, so it was impossible to give your full attention to any one of them. That is frustrating and unfortunate. When too much is going on, there is no way each effort can be carried out in an excellent manner. And the problem affects more than those in leadership.

The very people we hope to serve get short-changed when we cannot maintain high quality in our ministry efforts. The impact on their lives is diminished, and their eagerness to invite others is radically reduced. In short, by attempting to do too much—even with the best of motives—we actually run the risk of doing less.

It is painfully obvious that none of us has the ability to do everything. Yet if we looked at our schedules, one might think we believed otherwise. Have you ever wanted to surgically remove some ministry obligations from your schedule? Think about this: if those of us in leadership feel overloaded, how much more do the people in our ministries feel that way?

Perhaps by doing fewer, yet more strategically planned, programs we might make a greater impact and at the same time protect our most precious resource—our people. To some extent leaders should protect the time and energy of their people. By doing fewer things and doing them well we might also provide our people the time they need for their families and for building relationships with non-Christians.

A Breath of Fresh Air

If you have been in a position of leadership very long at all, the last thing you need is more work added to the "To Do" pile. This book is intended to be a journey of rediscovery, not the burden of more work. Focused and purposeful programming is a key to keeping ministry manageable. It is not merely a good idea; it was the method of the Master Himself.

Enjoy the fresh air that flows from a rediscovered sense of purpose. Enjoy the rest that comes from knowing that everything doesn't have to be done right now. And apply your discoveries. Apply the principles of the disciple-making process to your ministry. Do not be surprised if you find yourself thinking, *This seems too simple. It sounds too easy.* There is an amazing simplicity about the ministry of Christ, which we hope to help you discover as you seek to build a discipling strategy for your church.

Notes

1. Andrew Kuyvenhoven, "Declining Church Attendance," *Faith Today,* September/October 1990, p. 15.
2. Aubrey Malphurs, "Why Are Fewer and Fewer People Going to Church Today and What Can We Do About It?" *Kindred Spirit,* Spring 1990, pp. 3ff.
3. Donald McGavran, quoted in ibid.
4. Ed Erny, "Beyond the Hammer and Sickle—The Crescent," *OMS Outreach,* September/October 1990, p. 9.
5. George Barna, *The Frog in the Kettle: What Christians Need to Know About Life in the Year 2000* (Ventura, Calif.: Regal, 1990), p. 45.

3

CHRIST, OUR EXAMPLE

Behold I bring you good news of a great joy which shall be for all the people; for today in the city of David there has been born for you a Savior, who is Christ the Lord" (Luke 2:10-11, NASB). Such was the announcement made by angels at the birth of Jesus. Every aspect of His life, teaching, death, and resurrection was to be *good news* for a world in need of a Savior. There was never any aspect of life or ministry that He touched without bringing good news into the situation.

This good news extends to leaders in His church. We do not need to grope through dark and murky waters searching for obscure secrets of ministry. "Giving our all for the Master" does not compel us to run around frantically in every direction trying to meet every need until we reach the point of exhaustion. In Christ we have the good news of clear purpose fleshed out for us clearly. By observing the example of Christ we can observe the pattern that will enable us to accomplish His desires. This is not just good news—it is *great* news!

Jesus was very careful and deliberate in developing His ministry. He never tried to do everything. He never appeared rushed or pressured by a schedule that was out of control. He was content to move on to new locations even while crowds were anxious for Him to remain. At one point He was willing to wait until a friend had been dead four days before intervening, and then said the delay was so that God would be glorified (John

11:4). At every point His actions were determined by His purpose and His priorities.

We have already discussed the fact that the Great Commission is intended to be the purpose that drives the church. And we have wrestled with the kind of ministry that fulfills the Great Commission—a ministry able to meet people wherever they are spiritually. These convictions have come to life by studying the strategy of Jesus' own ministry. He is our example, and the approach He took in building His ministry is the basis for this entire book.

In his classic book *The Master Plan of Evangelism,* Robert Coleman expressed the genius of Christ's ministry model.

> His life was ordered by His objective. Everything He did and said was a part of the whole pattern. It had significance because it contributed to the ultimate purpose of His life in redeeming the world for God. This was the motivating vision governing His behavior. His steps were ordered by it. Mark it well. Not for one moment did Jesus lose sight of His goal.
>
> That is why it is so important to observe the way Jesus maneuvered to achieve His objective. *The Master disclosed God's strategy of world conquest.* He had confidence in the future precisely because He lived according to that plan in the present. There was nothing haphazard about His life—no wasted energy, not an idle word. He was on business for God (Luke 2:49). He lived, He died, and He rose again according to schedule. Like a general plotting His course of battle, the Son of God calculated to win. He could not afford to take a chance. Weighing every alternative and variable factor in human experience, He conceived a plan that would not fail. (Italics added)[1]

What was that "strategy of world conquest"? Answering that question is the purpose of this chapter. Before we go any further we need to study the example of the Master and take a close look at His strategy. There is deliberate order and development to His ministry. What He did do, what He did not do, and when He did it reveal that strategy. When you look closely at His work you find order and natural development in it.

THE MASTER'S STRATEGY

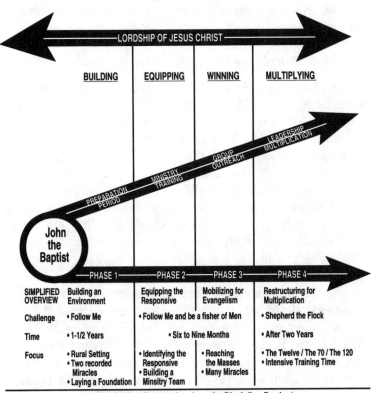

	BUILDING	EQUIPPING	WINNING	MULTIPLYING
	PHASE 1	PHASE 2	PHASE 3	PHASE 4
SIMPLIFIED OVERVIEW	Building an Environment	Equipping the Responsive	Mobilizing for Evangelism	Restructuring for Multiplication
Challenge	• Follow Me	• Follow Me and be a fisher of Men		• Shepherd the Flock
Time	• 1-1/2 Years	• Six to Nine Months		• After Two Years
Focus	• Rural Setting • Two recorded Miracles • Laying a Foundation	• Identifying the Responsive • Building a Minsitry Team	• Reaching the Masses • Many Miracles	• The Twelve / The 70 / The 120 • Intensive Training Time

The Biblical Process Leads to the Discipling Product

Hopefully, in this process of observation you will find your own passions and convictions to carry on the ministry of Christ encouraged and inflamed. In subsequent chapters we will try to apply the principles of Jesus' strategy to our own ministries. For now, let's take a short journey through the different phases of Jesus' ministry.

PHASE 1—BUILDING A FOUNDATION

A typical perception of Jesus' ministry is that He officially called, or appointed, the twelve disciples very early. In fact, many people believe that appointing the twelve was one of the first things Christ did. Although it is true that a few of the apostles began to follow Him during the early days, Jesus did not formally appoint the twelve until much later. The first phase of Jesus' public ministry was really a preparation period. It was a time in which He devoted Himself to building the foundation that would nurture and sustain significant growth. This period lasted for as long as eighteen to twenty-one months. [2]

During this phase, Jesus made short trips to various sections of the country. Yet it appears that He focused on the rural, less populated areas of Judea. Some events of this period are familiar: Jesus was baptized by John and endured the wilderness temptations, He cleansed the Temple for the first time, met the Samaritan woman, and taught Nicodemus. The culmination of this preparation period occurred at the synagogue in Nazareth when He announced that He was the embodiment of Isaiah's words. Note that only two specific miracles are recorded during this entire time—the wedding miracle at Cana and the healing of the nobleman's son.

Although we could spend a great deal of time discussing these events, our purpose here is to examine the patterns and broad strokes of the ministry of Christ. What were the emphases in His teaching? With whom did He spend time? How did He teach them?

In light of His desire to build a healthy foundation, it is not surprising to see a major emphasis on Jesus' identity here. Each of the gospel writers, as well as Jesus Himself, devoted considerable attention to helping people understand who He was (see passages on His birth, words of John the Baptist before and at Jesus' baptism, and Jesus' discourses with Nicodemus and the Samaritan woman in John 3-4). Understanding His identity is the basis for personal belief in Jesus as the Savior. Whereas John the Baptist emphasized repentance in light of coming judgment, Jesus preached repentance and *belief* (Mark 1:15).

What about the people Jesus taught and spent time with? Although we have a tendency to view each episode in Jesus' life as an independent event, an interesting pattern is evident when you look at the whole. In every circumstance Jesus' habit was to go where the people were. Do not miss this! His emphasis on going to people, as opposed to waiting for people to come to Him, is a crucial aspect of His strategy. He was reaching out to anyone and everyone with whom He came in contact. He was trying to build relationships with as many as possible. "Come and follow Me" was His challenge.

As He taught and spent time with people He also made it a habit to seek out those who were responsive. Clearly Jesus was always on the lookout for those who were responsive to Him and to His message. To those people He devoted extra attention (John 3:22). His formal appointment of the twelve disciples later was an extension of this pattern.

In any ministry there is a need to lay the right foundation, to create a healthy environment, and to establish patterns. Jesus took the time to do that. He not only built His ministry perfectly, but in so doing He demonstrated some of the very things we need to focus our own energies on.

When you think about the magnitude of the work Jesus came to do, it is incredible that He spent so much time laying a foundation. He had so little time yet so many things to teach.

There were so many people to train and so many lost without a savior. Yet with perfect wisdom and patience He carried out a flawless plan.

We have much to learn from Him about the process of building a ministry. Never be too hasty to move away from building and maintaining a foundation. Beware of the lure of those things that lie ahead. The important goals and needs before you can consume you and lead you prematurely away from the foundation of your ministry.

PHASE 2—EQUIPPING A TEAM

Jesus' rejection at Nazareth marked a turning point in His ministry. Following that precarious experience in the midst of the crowd on the cliff, Jesus moved to what we might call a new headquarters for His ministry, in Capernaum. However, something even more significant occurred at this point. He specifically called the first five disciples: Peter, Andrew, James, John, and Matthew (Matt. 4:18-22).[3]

Until this point, as we have already observed, Jesus made it His habit to seek all kinds of people from all kinds of backgrounds. Now He paid particular attention to those who were responsive to Him. He had seen that responsiveness in those He called to be His disciples. Now He called them not only to follow Him but to receive special training. He promised to help them become "fishers of men" (Matt. 4:19; Mark 1:17) and in so doing inaugurated what we might call an "equipping" or "ministry training" phase of ministry.

You are certainly familiar with many of the well-known events that took place during this six- to nine-month phase of Jesus' ministry. It was during this time that Peter's mother-in-law was healed, a leper was cleansed, the paralytic was healed, and a series of Sabbath controversies took place. However, in addition to these familiar episodes, the equipping of a few in order to multiply the ministry was one of Christ's overriding concerns.

Although we who are leaders in the church today are prone to be slow learners and fast forgetters, Jesus was able to keep His strategy for ministry in perfect focus. He knew what Moses didn't realize until his father-in-law pointed it out: that the load of ministry leadership is far too great for any one person to carry alone. Jesus knew what Paul would write of later, that the primary role of leadership is to equip others to do the work of the ministry (Eph. 4:11-12). Jesus knew that there comes a time when those who have been growing need to be challenged, stretched, and trained to serve others. He put His energies into establishing a team that could share the work of the ministry.

As they traveled with Jesus those men received special training in a number of areas. Much of their training occurred while they were traveling. As they walked with Jesus, they were able to discuss all that they had heard and seen. At every corner they learned of the Master's priorities. They saw how He loved people, even the unlovely and the sinful. They witnessed His ability to heal and to forgive. In every miracle their understanding of His authority was stretched until no area of life was left uncovered. And in the controversies over the Sabbath they were forced to reevaluate what it meant to please God.

Many of us verbally affirm the need to be equippers. We champion the cry for the entire Body of Christ to become active in ministry. We beg people to be more than mere spectators of the ministry—for their own sakes! Yet have we learned the lessons about equipping others as demonstrated by Jesus Himself? Before moving on to phase 3, pause to ask yourself an important question: Are there men or women in your ministry who are ready for more? Are some people ready to be trained as workers and multipliers?

PHASE 3—WINNING THE MASSES

Having built a base or foundation for His ministry and having called out a ministry team, Jesus now began to mobilize that team for evangelism. Although we are calling the outreach aspect of Jesus' ministry a separate phase, it is really part and parcel of the equipping process. What we now call the Great Commission was being modeled to the disciples so that their hearts would beat like His for the lost. Jesus was nurturing a Great Commission passion in those men long before He stated it in a succinct transferable form.

Allow Mark to give you a feel for the outreach during this phase (1:14–2:12). Soon after Jesus chose the first five team members He traveled to Capernaum and got down to business. He began preaching to the crowds in the synagogue. He drove a demon from a man. Then in Peter's home, after Jesus healed Peter's mother-in-law, Mark says the whole town gathered at the door. The response was phenomenal, but the point is that this is a new phase in His ministry.

At this point of great popularity Jesus teaches His disciples an important lesson about evangelism. It is not enough to have great response from a few. People are lost and in need of the Savior in other places as well. Refusing to be influenced by the clamor of the crowd, Jesus left Capernaum and took His followers throughout Galilee, preaching in synagogues everywhere.

In this phase Jesus moved aggressively into outreach to the masses. He preached everywhere and performed many miracles. His outreach methodology had a twofold purpose. First and foremost, He was working to reach the masses. Jesus was passionately burdened for the lost and sought to reach out to people everywhere He went.

His second purpose was to model the process and involve His ministry team in outreach. He wanted His disciples to share His passion, and He wanted to give them the ability to duplicate His ministry. His desire was to help them succeed in the task of evangelism. He knew the result in their lives would be both deep joy as well as lifelong conviction and commitment to Great Commission living.

Do you notice any difference at this point from the usual methodology in our own churches? Frequently we aim the majority of our efforts at Christians. Then we turn around and plead with people to share the gospel with their non-Christian acquaintances. But the average believer needs help in reaching out to others. Christ knew that! By taking along the men being trained for ministry He was giving them an example to follow. He was also helping them experience success in what He would later commission them to do.

No doubt you have a desire to reach the lost. But perhaps some of the genius of Christ's strategy was that as a leader He helped His people succeed in the task of evangelism. Rather than just talk about evangelism, He led the way in creating avenues of group success. This aspect of our Savior's strategy should be reflected in the corporate strategy of every ministry and every church. We have learned how to teach people the words of the gospel message. Now it is time to learn how to get involved together in bringing that message to the masses of our generation.

PHASE 4—RESTRUCTURING FOR MULTIPLICATION

About two and a half years into His ministry Jesus formally appointed the twelve, whom He called apostles. Jesus' ministry had grown, and the increased numbers of people made it necessary to appoint leadership to allow the ministry to multiply. The twelve had been with Jesus from the beginning. They had come to trust Him as their Messiah. They had been involved with Him in ministry training and outreach, and now they were ready for shepherding responsibilities. This was another step in their growth and another example of Jesus' pattern of identifying those who were responsive.

The selection and appointment process went something like this. After spending an entire night in prayer Jesus gathered His disciples on a mountain near Galilee. There He called out twelve whom He identified as "apostles" (see Matt. 10:1;

Mark 3:13-19; Luke 6:12-19). It appears that the Sermon on the Mount may well have been an ordination sermon of sorts (Luke 6:12-16).

Training for these newly appointed leaders appears to have involved a basic format: teaching, showing, sending, and involving. You can see this plan at work immediately after the twelve were appointed. *Teaching*—the Sermon on the Mount would have been the first formal discourse for this leadership team (Luke 7:1a). *Showing*—after His discourse, Jesus took the leaders on a ministry trip to Capernaum in order to demonstrate what He had just taught them (Luke 7:1b). *Sending*—He then sent out the twelve to do the work of the ministry, just as He had done (Luke 9:1-6). Later, He did the very same thing with the seventy. *Involving*—Jesus also involved them in His ministry to the masses. They became co-laborers with Him (Luke 9:11-17).

As Christ's ministry continued to expand, He recognized the need to appoint leaders to allow the ministry to multiply. So Jesus looked over the ministry team He had been equipping, chose twelve that had proved themselves to be faithful and able workers, and began to train them to shepherd a segment of the flock. He continued to train them and intensively invested His life in them. At this point in Christ's ministry things began to mushroom.

These four phases of Jesus' ministry line up with the four types of programming suggested in chapter 2. Phase 1 corresponds with growth level programming. Phase 2 lays the framework for ministry training, and phase 3 begins a corporate outreach effort. The process of establishing a solid ministry leads us to a balanced winning, building, equipping product.

Christ models the process of establishing a discipling product. That's why Jesus could boldly say, "As the Father has sent Me, I also send you" (John 20:21).

As one well-known educator said, "How can we learn? How did Jesus Christ train His men? Whenever we study the gospels we tend to study them exclusively for content. Why don't we study them for methodology?"[4] Often when we study the life of Christ we look only at the overall message. We do need to address His overall methodology as well. Christ's methods reflect the divine priorities of His Great Commission.

Whether you serve in a ministry to students, a work with singles, a parachurch organization, or as pastor of a church, the pattern of Jesus' ministry reflects God's blueprint for your ministry. This strategy was Jesus' perfect way to make disciples with a Great Commission vision. In taking the time to build a ministry through these four phases, He developed people who were able to multiply His ministry long after He was gone. Can we afford to settle for less?

The message of the gospel is incredibly good news, and Jesus' method of ministry is also good news for the weary leader. In the chapters to follow, we will explore the implications of His methods for local ministry.

Notes

1. Robert E. Coleman, *The Master Plan of Evangelism* (Old Tappan, N.J.: Revell, 1964), p. 18.

2. The timetable used as a reference for the chronology of the Life of Christ is found in *A Harmony of the Gospels*, by Robert L. Thomas and Stanley N. Gundry (Chicago: Moody, 1978), p. 348.

3. There was an additional call of the four recorded in Luke 5:1-11. Matthew's call is recorded in 9:9, Mark 2:13-14, and Luke 5:27-28 but appears to have taken place during this period when harmonized with Mark and Luke.

4. Howard Hendricks, "Discussing First Things First," *Leadership*, Summer 1980, p. 106.

SECTION 2

How Do We Get There?

"HEY, IF YOU GUYS WOULD GET OFF YOUR KNEES LONG ENOUGH, I COULD TEACH YOU SOMETHING ABOUT CHURCH GROWTH."

PHASE 1

BUILDING A FOUNDATION

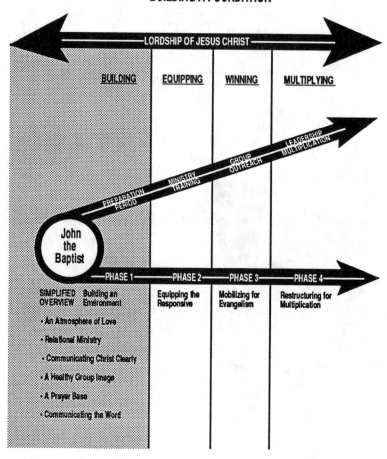

4

AN ENVIRONMENT FOR GROWTH

There is a beautiful area in northern California known as the wine country. Immaculately groomed vineyards stretch on for miles and miles in startling symmetry. Yet each vineyard grows its own particular varieties of grapes according to its own specific standards. The processing facilities of each vineyard differ from others by virtue of capacity as well as heritage. Some use old world processes and have a unique beauty about them. Others are high tech operations, mixing the lessons of the past with discoveries of the present. But all of them rely on one indispensable factor.

Each vintner is dependent on the right kind of climate for the growing of his grapes. In fact, precisely because the factors of climate are just right, this section of California has become a well-known wine producing region. The same is true of every other famous wine region in the world. It is even true that some regions specialize in one type of wine specifically because their particular climate grows certain grapes better than any other.

Growing good grapes requires more than good stock and willing laborers. Good grapes are produced when good vines are planted in good soil and then nurtured in the right environment. That environment, or climate, includes appropriate sunshine, suitable temperatures, and the right amount of humidity.

All of these factors in the right proportions create an environment for maximum growth.

In the same way, Christians do not automatically grow up in Christ. They need to be in an environment that adequately fosters and nurtures growth. Leadership cannot make growth happen; it is God who causes growth (1 Cor. 3:6). Much as the right climate enables grapes to grow into perfection, the church needs to create an environment that will help people grow. Building this kind of "climate" is exactly what Jesus did during the first phase of His ministry.

Perhaps as much as half of Jesus' formal ministry years were devoted to building an environment that would produce disciples. He knew that certain fundamentals must be established and continually cultivated in order for His followers to be nurtured. He knew that a discipling ministry with a heart for the Great Commission is built on, empowered by, and sustained by an environment that effectively helps believers grow. His pattern, as always, is a model for us.

BACK TO THE BASICS

Based on the example of Christ we would like to suggest six foundational aspects of ministry that are crucial to creating an environment for growth. Leadership's task is to instigate, refine, and continually enhance the quality of these elements of ministry. Each of the following six priorities will be discussed at length in later chapters. For now, a thumbnail sketch of each will serve to paint an overall picture.

1. CREATE AN ATMOSPHERE OF LOVE

The biblical mandate to create a spirit of love within the Body of Christ is pervasive. Biblically and sociologically we can see clear evidence of the powerful impact of love on people's lives. Jesus' insight, "By this will all men know that [we] are [his] disciples if [we] love one another," has never been more true (John 13:35). The challenge for leaders is to lead the way in developing an environment of love.

2. BUILD A RELATIONAL MINISTRY

Perhaps one of the most arresting aspects of the ministry of Jesus was His pattern of going *to* people, not merely waiting for them to come to Him. During Phase 1, Jesus relied heavily upon this priority as He "spent time with His disciples" (John 3:22). Building relationships with people was an intentional, aggressive agenda for Christ. He knew of the need and lived by the principle that people respond when we reach out to them, as opposed to our telling them to come to us. Everything we do in ministry is geared toward people—toward the goal of impacting individuals. The stage is set for this kind of ministry when we adopt an aggressive approach to building relationships.

3. COMMUNICATE CHRIST CLEARLY

Leaders must constantly evaluate how well we are presenting Christ. In a world that knows only caricatures of Christ, people need to know Him as He really is. We must present Him as He is and present His message of life and grace as He gave it. Our challenge is to continually communicate the Person and work of Christ in a clear manner so that people might build a real relationship with the living Savior.

4. BUILD A HEALTHY MINISTRY IMAGE

The image that people have of the ministry they participate in has a direct impact on a number of key things. Cohesiveness, commitment to the cause, receptivity to change, and even teachability are all related to a healthy group image. What kind of vision do the people in your ministry have for the work to which God has called them? How confident are they in His ability to accomplish the task which He has entrusted to their hands? Creating a healthy image of your ministry among your people is a foundational task that benefits almost every aspect of your ministry.

5. MOBILIZE A PRAYER BASE

Our task is to effect spiritual life change—nothing more, nothing less. However, this kind of spiritual work is not accomplished by human means. As we move into the arena of prayer, God moves into the arena of our lives. He has chosen to act in response to the prayers of His people. Everyone in leadership within the Body of Christ is anxious for God to do the supernatural. We recognize the reality of the spiritual warfare in which we and our people are involved. Yet, prayer—substantial and aggressive prayer—is frequently one of those things we "run out of time" for. Individually, as well as corporately, we need to increase our prayer base.

6. COMMUNICATE THE WORD

Research has shown that even our most regular churchgoers have some illiteracy in the Word. Could it be that we talk a lot about the Word but rarely get people into it? We continually need to evaluate our own teaching and the prevalent teaching in our ministries to insure that God's Word is being taught accurately. We also need to be cautious against allowing our zeal for changed lives to cause us to use the Word as a club to straighten people out. It is not difficult to lose the message of grace under a message of "God says you have to . . . " Those in leadership need to set an example of opening the Word in a manner that helps people discover what it says as well as how to apply it to their lives.

KEEPING YOUR HEAD CLEAR

That list of ministry essentials is not revolutionary. It shouldn't be! Yet the very familiarity we have with those concepts can be the problem. We find it easy to leave those things which seem elementary or basic and move on to those which might appear to be more challenging. Most of us have felt the temptation to move on to newer programs at the expense of basic priorities. Fight that temptation! These six basic building blocks of ministry are so crucial that none of us can afford to cease cultivating them. Regardless of what happens, our ministries will never grow beyond their need for these essentials.

It would be nice if we could all begin afresh and make these six foundational practices a consuming focus from the beginning. You probably don't have that luxury. However, it is never too late to redirect your attentions. As you are able to build these efforts into the core of your activities, it will be like strengthening the structural beams of your ministry. You can expect certain benefits. And there are certain cautions you should keep in mind as well.

BENEFITS TO EXPECT

People growing in Christ. People at every level of spiritual maturity benefit from the environment created by these six priorities. It may seem too simple, but don't be fooled. The process of growing in Christ is indeed fairly simple, although not simplistic.

Fuel for our ministries. More and more it seems that church leaders are frustrated by the lack of workers to serve and lead ministry efforts. People are the fuel of our ministries—our most priceless resource. When they are fed by an environment that nurtures them and helps them grow, they become available for service. They serve with the eagerness that comes from a full spirit.

Room to expand. These six priorities function much like the foundation and superstructure of a building. The deeper and stronger the foundation, the greater the building it will support. Everyone in ministry leadership has a desire to expand their impact in the community and in the people God has placed in their hands. Building an adequate foundation will enable you to expand. In fact, as you continue to cultivate these practices you should experience a continually expanding base for ministry.

CAUTIONS TO KEEP IN MIND

Simply forgetting. Perhaps the greatest warning is to be careful about simply forgetting to cultivate these essentials. Sometimes the familiar priorities are the easiest to forget or take for granted when everything else gets hectic. When you have worked hard to establish these essentials, stay with them. They are the key ingredients to an environment that will nourish people.

The "lure of success" syndrome. For whatever reason, we are accustomed to measuring ministry success by the three B's: buildings, bucks, and bodies. We think that if our ministry is growing in any of these—and hopefully all of them—we are certainly experiencing success. There is nothing wrong with growth in these areas. In many cases they *are* tangible evidence of progress. However, there is a not-so-subtle lure for any leader to focus his efforts on progress in one or more of these areas, even at the expense of more fundamental efforts.

The Tyranny of the Urgent. Do you remember Charles Hummel's powerful little booklet by this title? A real problem for anyone in leadership is that important needs do not always demand immediate attention. Hummel writes:

> Your greatest danger is letting the urgent things crowd out the important. The important task rarely must be done today, or even this week. But the urgent tasks call for instant action. The momentary appeal of these tasks seems irresistible and important. But, in light of time's perspective their deceptive prominence fades; with a sense of loss we recall the important task pushed aside.[1]

Most of those six priorities of a nurturing environment will never scream out, demanding immediate attention. Yet neglecting them will erode the environment of growth we so desperately need.

Leaders in the ministry of Christ need to tackle these priorities intentionally. They will serve you and your people well. Prevent anything from blocking them out of your life or ministry.

Note

1. Charles E. Hummel, *The Tyranny of the Urgent,* 10th ed. (Downers Grove, Ill.: Inter-Varsity Christian Fellowship, 1977), pp. 4-5.

5

AN ATMOSPHERE OF LOVE

By this all men will know that you are my disciples.
—John 13:35

L ove. Many of us have a love-hate relationship with the very word itself. Few words carry such significance or can move you so deeply. At one moment it conveys tremendous positive emotion. In another, the mere mention of the word can make you nauseous. Covering the gamut from marketing superficiality to self-sacrificial commitment, *love* is a word that crops up in every aspect of our lives.

Separate yourself from the familiarity—or inundation—of the greeting card variety of love. Such familiarity breeds a dangerous callousness to the concept of love even within the Body of Christ, but Jesus does not allow us the option of being complacent. He placed a premium on love as an essential quality to be nurtured in the lives of His disciples and in the corporate life of His church. Perhaps one of the best ways to personalize the priority of love is to examine the life of a man transformed by the love of Christ.

THE TRANSFORMING POWER OF LOVE

From his earliest memories the smell of fish and the sounds of the fishing trade marked the place he called home. The life and folklore of the fishing village where he grew up

were woven into the fabric of his home. His father was a prominent fisherman in partnership with another man from the area.
His boyhood was filled with adventures among the nets, fresh
fish, and old boats along the water's edge. Although there was
always plenty of activity and excitement, the environment did
not provide the best setting for the moral development of children. The talk and swagger of the sailors peppered the speech
of every boy in town.

John was not much different from other men in town. As a
matter of fact, he epitomized the gruff, swarthy, macho man of
the sea recognized around the world. Able to hold his own in
any scuffle and marked by the scars of many personal skir-
mishes, he had quite a reputation. "Sons of Thunder"—that's
what Jesus called him and his brother (Mark 3:17).

We know John and his brother James as apostles. We
know them as pillars of the church, men who carried the truth
of Christ into a pagan world. The early church looked to them
for direction and example. They clarified for all Christians what
it meant to live in relationship with Jesus Christ. John, in particular, was called upon by God to write five of the books we now
have in our New Testament. This "Son of Thunder" has been
referred to as the apostle of love because his writings are filled
with references to love.

Think about the transformation of John's life. You cannot
help but be struck by an overwhelming appreciation for the
power of love. Given their nickname, John and his brother were
not exactly the tenderhearted type. On one occasion they were
so upset that they wanted Jesus to wipe out a whole Samaritan
village. They were enraged because a town of Samaritans
would not put them up for the night. In modern day language
they cried out, "Let's toast 'em, Jesus!" It may sound funny,
but they were sincerely suggesting that Jesus call down fire and
destroy those people (Luke 9:51-56)!

On other occasions John and his brother tried to wheel
and deal with Jesus for privileged positions in heaven. "Jesus, if
we ask You for a favor, would You promise to give it to us?

Promise us that when we get to heaven the two of us can sit in the seats of highest honor. We want to sit right next to You!" (see Mark 10:35-37). Does that sound like a servant's heart to you?

Clearly John and his brother had more than their share of rough edges. Only Jesus in His perfect wisdom could have seen the potential in these men. Yet, it is John more than any other writer of the New Testament who challenges us to love one another. It is John who records most of Christ's teaching on the importance of love. John writes so much about love because he knew about the transforming power of love firsthand.

Jesus understood the transforming power of love well. He calls us to love one another because of the results it can produce. The people whom God has called you to serve are desperate for love. They don't need that mushy, fuzzy, spineless ooze but the meaty compassion and commitment that we see in Christ. In John we see a glimpse of love's power, and throughout Scripture we read of its importance.

THE PRIORITY OF LOVE

The priority of love is a clarion call throughout Scripture. Jesus' well known words, as recorded by John, summarize this mandate in a succinct and penetrating fashion: "A new command I give you: Love one another. As I have loved you, so you must love one another. By this all men will know that you are my disciples, if you love one another" (John 13:34-35).

And this command is heard in different forms. Moses, recording the law for Israel, wrote, "Love your neighbor as yourself" (Lev. 19:18). Peter writes to the believers scattered throughout Asia Minor, "Above all, love each other deeply, because love covers a multitude of sins" (1 Pet. 4:8). The author of Hebrews instructs us to set as a personal habit the goal of "[stimulating] one another to love and good deeds" (Heb. 10:24, NASB). Perhaps Paul's words to Timothy are the clearest in laying out the priority of leaders to develop love: "The goal of our instruction is love from a pure heart and a good conscience and a sincere faith" (1 Tim. 1:5, NASB).

Could the biblical case be stronger? Look closely at a few of these passages, and reflect on their impact in your ministry. First Peter 4 is one of the most intriguing. Most of us have attended a number of churches and participated in different ministry efforts. Have you noticed the difference between those places where people truly loved one another and those where they didn't? Where there is a lack of love there seems to be a multitude of sins: accusations, innuendos, gossip, political infighting, and so on. This principle is even more apparent among junior high or high school students. If you have ever attended a retreat with a group of students that did not love one another you were witness to—and perhaps victim of—a multitude of sins. But the group that truly loves each other is a place of tolerance, encouragement, and dramatic spiritual growth.

Hebrews 10 calls us to stimulate love in one another. The Lord does not say, "It would be nice if you could all become a bit more congenial." His message instead is that helping one another put love into action is a major priority for all Christians. Paul's strong statement to Timothy tells us that leaders are to be consciously pursuing this goal. "The overwhelming testimony of the New Testament is that love both expressed and experienced among members of the body is absolutely essential if that body is to be healthy and alive. Thus the development of love within the body must be a primary concern of the spiritual leadership."[1]

Does this discussion about creating an atmosphere of love make sense? Do you understand it to be a primary task of those who lead the Body of Christ?

These passages and almost fifty others in the New Testament reiterate the priority of love. It is absolutely clear that believers need to grow in love, but they also need love to grow. The task of leaders is to do all we can to create a place where love is genuinely expressed. Creating a place where people are loved is a priority in Scripture, and it is a drastic need within our culture.

THE DESPERATE NEED FOR LOVE

He has been referred to as "the Love Doctor." His lectures are packed. In fact, Leo Buscalia has become well known across the country for his talks on why and how we might learn to love each other. Lecturing—preaching really—he works up a sweat telling story after story of the need for and power of love.

Has Leo Buscalia discovered a previously unknown secret to better human relationships? Hardly. What he has done is to pinpoint a major need that people have and then given them something to do about it. Through simple illustrations about listening, touching, hugging, caring, and so on, Dr. Buscalia connects with a deep desire in every person to love and be loved.

We don't need to alter the simple message of the gospel. We have no need to rewrite the agenda of the church into a warm and fuzzy touchy-feely session. However, the church is intended to be a place where the love of Christ is known. Today, as much or more than in any other generation, people are hurting and in desperate need of sincere love. Even where all of the external fixtures of life appear intact, people are bleeding and weary on the inside.

You know the grim statistics. You also know the personal tragedies of those to whom you minister. There is a strange dichotomy at work in our world. On the one hand, it seems as if more and more people are hurting. Whether the cause is job-related, divorce, abuse, or drugs, there seems to be an ever increasing level of personal pain in our society. On the other hand, there is an increasing level of selfishness. In spite of the fact that love is the thing we need the most, it is the thing we give the least. The kind of love that would make a difference—the others-oriented, giving kind of love that Jesus spoke of—is rare.

Yet the words of Jesus echo louder and louder all the time. "By this all men will know that you are my disciples, if you love one another." When we demonstrate the love of Christ, the gospel comes to life for those around us. They see in us, individually and corporately, a quality not found elsewhere. We become a torch showing a way of hope in a dark world. The love that Christ has for a lost world takes on flesh and bones through our love for one another. It could be said that every aspect of the work that Christ desires to do is enhanced by genuine love.

LOVE IN ACTION

1 Corinthians 13 has been called "the love chapter" and rightly so. In the span of only thirteen verses the apostle Paul unfolds the meaning and even some of the mystery of real love. In verses 4-7 he gives us a list of the ways love acts. Catch this: every action on this list benefits other people. Every item stands out as a bright light in stark contrast to the way people are treated every day in the world.

Joe Aldrich wrote a powerful book titled *Lifestyle Evangelism.* He suggests playing the music of the gospel in order to prepare someone for the words of the gospel.[2] The kind of love defined for us in 1 Corinthians 13 does play that "music of the gospel." It sings a sweet, refreshing song that people long to hear. Look over this list and ask, What would our ministry look like if these ingredients of love were the regular course of action? If people were treated with the kind of love that . . .

> Never fails?
> Is always kind?
> Does not get envious?
> Does not boast?
> Is not rude?
> Is not proud?

Is not self-seeking, self-serving?
Does not anger easily?
Keeps no record of wrongs?
Does not take delight in another person's evil?
Rejoices with the truth?
Always protects?
Always trusts?
Always hopes?
Always perseveres?

With that kind of love, people would recognize the work of real life change. It creates a thirst for more—a thirst to taste the source of that love. It creates a platform to explain the love of the Savior who makes it possible.

Genuine love makes a compelling contribution to the process of evangelism, but it also enhances the growth process. Ephesians 4:15 tells us that love is a catalyst that sparks growth. "Speaking the truth in love, we will in all things grow up into him who is the Head, that is, Christ."

Teachers and preachers of the Word wish to believe that our eloquent speaking skill is all that is needed to effect life-change in people. We know in our hearts it is not true because we understand our utter dependence on the work of the Spirit. But do we understand the essential component of love in the growth process? The degree to which we are effective in communicating love is the degree to which we will see our people grow in Jesus Christ.

STRATEGIES FOR CREATING AN ENVIRONMENT OF LOVE

Following are some ideas of how you might tangibly create an environment of love. Please understand, they are merely a starting point. You might want to gather together with other leaders in your church and brainstorm for additional ideas.

1. LOOK IN THE MIRROR

Every morning you undoubtedly look into your mirror to make sure all essential pieces are still present or accounted for. Some mornings this can be a disappointing experience. Yet it is an essential aspect of daily life. Self-evaluation in other areas is equally essential. For example, every person in leadership must take an honest look at himself and ask, "Do I truly love these people?"

One principle of leadership states, "You cannot lead people in a direction you are not willing to go." So the first step in developing an environment of love in your ministry is to check your own attitude. Do you really love your people? When you are away from them, do you miss them? Is your work among them merely a duty, a job to fulfill, or is it the outgrowth of a compelling desire to serve them?

There is also a second issue. How well are you able to communicate love? You see, some of us can experience a boatload of feelings internally and yet do a poor job communicating them to others. Maybe you communicate love well one-on-one but poorly in a large group. Maybe vice versa. Seek out the insight and advice of others. Ask those who know you to be honest with you and tell you how well you communicate love. Ask them to give you ideas about how you might improve. This is such a crucial area that we cannot afford to settle for status quo. As Paul said, "In fact, you do love all the brothers. . . . Yet we urge you . . . to do so more and more" (1 Thess. 4:10).

It has often been said that the degree to which we are effective in communicating love is the degree to which we can see lives changed for Jesus Christ. The message "I love you, I care" must be said in many ways to our lonely and hurting world.

2. TEACH IN TONES OF LOVE, NOT LAW

Think about your teaching ministry in recent months. What attitude was presented about obedience? In our zeal for people to live for Christ, to live in obedience to Him, it is possible to subtly convey a message of performance-based acceptance.

Teaching in tones of law implies that in order to be acceptable to God we need to work harder. It says to do more of this or less of that. Yet this kind of teaching robs Christians of their joy. It produces Christians who constantly feel guilty about their imperfections. It can create an overbearing load of legalism and a general insecurity about one's position in Christ. And it does a gross injustice to the message of grace. Teaching in tones of law erodes an atmosphere of love and acceptance.

When we teach in tones of love, we start with a different premise. We start with the understanding that we are already completely accepted by Jesus Christ. Our acceptability is based on His work, not on our own. Our standing before God is based upon His performance, decidedly not our own. The position we have in Christ forms a basis for a different emphasis and different application of our teaching.

3. CULTIVATE GOOD LISTENING SKILLS

Paul Tournier pinpointed the crux of this issue when he said, "Listen to all the conversations of our world, those between nations as well as those between couples. They are for the most part dialogues of the deaf. Each one speaks primarily in order to set forth his own ideas, in order to justify himself, in order to enhance himself and to accuse others. Exceedingly few exchanges of viewpoints manifest a real desire to understand the other person."[3]

Few things communicate love like a patient, listening ear. When someone listens to you with undivided attention you instinctively know he cares about you. Listening carefully to another person is hard work. It requires abandoning your own mental agenda in order to pay attention to his. It requires thinking more about someone else's issues than your own potential responses. Listening is something most of us do poorly, and yet it is a potent way to demonstrate that we care. Cultivating the habit of listening to one another among those who are leaders in your ministry will yield an extraordinary return.

4. USE DISAPPOINTMENTS AS OPPORTUNITIES TO DEMONSTRATE GOD'S LOVE

Inevitably there will be days when you are disappointed by people. Perhaps someone falls through on a responsibility that he or she accepted. Or a difficult situation may be handled improperly. Or maybe the problem is interpersonal. Disappointments, whatever their cause, can be prime opportunities to demonstrate God's love.

Paul makes a case for this point in 2 Corinthians 2. Having dealt with a person who had caused them grief, Paul says it is now time to "forgive and comfort him." He says, "I urge you therefore, to reaffirm your love for him" (2 Cor. 2:5-8). When others disappoint us, we need to forgive them. Thus disappointments become opportunities to communicate that we love people for who they are, not what they do! In stark contrast to the world, which accepts people based on what they do, we can demonstrate love in the midst of disappointment.

5. CREATE OPPORTUNITIES WHERE LOVE CAN BE EXPRESSED

As obvious as this strategy sounds, it is surprisingly easy to overlook the need to create opportunities to express love. Intentionally planned times that allow people to express love to one another are very beneficial. In fact, the effort required to create specific opportunities to express love spills over and encourages spontaneous expressions of love.

Go to the Lord, and ask Him for ideas that would work well for your people. Ask Him to make you keenly aware of needs and opportunities that you might take advantage of. Maybe you could plan service projects where one group within the church could serve another. Maybe planned times of sharing in a Communion service would provide a good forum. Perhaps your small group studies or Sunday school classes could devote time to study and discuss the practice of loving one another. Maybe you could create ways for people to pray for one another. You should definitely consider including time during retreats to share and express love among your people.

6. PRAY

Ask God to create a spirit of love among your people and in your heart. Unfortunately prayer can become a perennial "also ran." Every good Christian agrees to its importance, and every leader in the Body of Christ encourages it. But prayer is not just a good idea on a long list. It is God's divine prescription for getting His work done. One aspect of His work is creating an atmosphere of love within your ministry, and as such it should be a priority for prayer. Creating an atmosphere of love is as dependent on the work of God Himself as anything else we try to do.

If the kind of change and growth we desire is a matter of attitude and will, and if God is the expert on performing internal change in people's lives, does it make any sense not to seek His work in wholehearted prayer? Ask Him to create genuine love within your ministry. Ask Him to begin His work in your own heart.

As you seek to effect changed lives, emphasize the priority of love. An environment of love provides a place where people can respond to and be changed by the truth of Jesus Christ. The apostle Paul knew this to be true when he wrote these words: "And now these three remain: faith, hope and love. But the greatest of these is love" (1 Cor. 13:13).

Notes

1. Larry Richards and Clyde Hoeldtke, *A Theology of Leadership* (Grand Rapids: Zondervan, 1981), p. 92.
2. Joseph Aldrich, *Lifestyle Evangelism* (Portland: Multnomah, 1981), pp. 77ff.
3. Paul Tournier, *To Understand Each Other* (Louisville, Ky.: John Knox, 1972), pp. 8-9.

6

RELATIONAL MINISTRY

You can impress people at a distance; you can only impact them up close. The general principle is this, the closer the personal relationship, the greater the potential for impact.

—Howard Hendricks

People usually do not trust those they do not know. In addition to a normal mistrust of the unknown, there is tremendous distrust in our day for organized religion. Some of this distrust is understandable. The media repeatedly aims its spotlight toward "religious" leaders who have fallen or have intentionally misled their followers. Regardless of the reasons, we need to be honest with ourselves about how we are perceived by the world around us.

In your heart your concern for people is genuine. You know that the message of the gospel is trustworthy. You know that your motives for ministry are pure. But in spite of your trustworthiness, the impact of mistrust on your ministry is staggering, because when you aren't trusted, you aren't listened to.

Put yourself in the shoes of the unchurched. Considering all the bad news you have seen paraded across your TV screen, why should you believe that the church has answers? What would make you change your mind about Christ and His church? What would break down your defensive barriers? After all, regardless of your interest in spiritual things, you have learned to keep Christians at bay with a few well-rehearsed remarks, such as, "Why should I go to church? The people there are no better than I am." Or, "Religious leaders don't care about me as a person; they are only interested in my money!" And, "I went to church once, and nobody even noticed me." "Why can't I get to know God my own way and avoid Christians—they are just hypocrites anyway."

Unfair as they might be, barriers of fear, misconception, and bad press are a reality. These barriers are effective insulators for people who are trying to stay away from the church. They are only broken down in the context of a relationship where trust has been earned. Aggressively seeking people in order to build relationships with them is the means of destroying fears that cause mistrust. In a relationship the unknown becomes known. True perceptions are fleshed out. And bad press is laid to rest in the light of personal integrity and authenticity.

Think about the example of Jesus. Things were not so different in His day. He knew it was essential to be aggressive in going to people. He was continually taking the first steps to initiate a relationship. Every step of the way He was getting involved with people. He established the priority of a relational ministry from the beginning. "After this, Jesus and his disciples went out into the Judean countryside, where he spent some time with them" (John 3:22). The need for relational ministry, felt so intensely today, has existed since the days of Christ and before.

THE MOVING EXAMPLE OF CHRIST

It had been an incredible day. In the morning Jesus had taught the crowds in the synagogue, ministered to those with needs, and spoken at length with many people. It had started out to be a very normal day. Upon leaving the synagogue He and His disciples went to Peter's home. They were probably hungry and in need of some peace and quiet after a busy morning.

However, when they arrived at Peter's home, plans quickly changed. Peter's mother-in-law was very ill. Immediately, Christ responded to her need and healed the disease infecting her body. Meanwhile, news of His arrival traveled throughout town and drew hundreds of people to Peter's home. Mark tells us that the "whole town" came to see Him. (Church planters would flip over such a response!)

It is easy to imagine that by this point the disciples, though tired, got fairly excited. People were responding to Jesus. The disciples had reorganized their priorities to follow Him, and now it was becoming apparent they had made a right choice. It looked as if they had certainly hitched their wagons to the right star. Witnessing the response of these crowds must have prompted the disciples to think, *This could be a perfect headquarters for Jesus' ministry. People from all over Israel could travel here to Capernaum to learn from Him.* Maybe Jesus would build His own synagogue near the lake. It all seemed perfect.

But that was not Jesus' method. After spending the early part of the next morning in prayer, Jesus informed His disciples that it was time to move on. "Let us go somewhere else—to the nearby villages—so I can preach there also. That is why I have come" (Mark 1:38).

His last words carried the punch. He had come with the specific priority of going to people everywhere. He would never set up camp in one location so that people would have to seek Him. Jesus was in the business of seeking others. It was His intention to aggressively take the initiative in building relational bridges. He was committed to seeking people Himself.

Examples abound in the gospels of Jesus doing exactly what He said that day in Capernaum. He was continually going where people were. In simple terms, the incarnation was God coming among men. His compassion for the individual never wavered. Jesus' encounter with Zacchaeus is a classic example. There was an unpopular, undesirable, unethical little tax collector hiding in a tree. Jesus had every opportunity to ignore him. He could have easily walked right on past. He could have dismissed him as a short man who simply wanted a better view. Instead, Jesus went out of His way to reach out to Zacchaeus and acknowledge his value as a person. Jesus asked for the chance to be a guest in His home. He cared about Zacchaeus and showed it by His eagerness to be with him (Luke 19:5).

Jesus' effort to build relationships with people was such a prominent pattern in His life that His enemies tried to use it to discredit Him. Our old friends the Pharisees wagged their fingers and hurled their insults saying, "Why does your teacher eat with tax collectors and sinners? Why—(insert an audible and snooty "hrumpf" here) he openly welcomes them!" (see Matt. 9:11; Luke 15:2). Actually the joke's on them. What they intended as a brutal accusation was in reality an affirming compliment. Jesus might have responded, "Why, gentlemen, thank you for noticing."

The point is that the ministry of Christ was a relational ministry. His strategy was appropriate not only for Him, it needs to be our strategy, too. If Jesus needed to devote time and energy to reaching out to people, how can we not do the same? Regardless of the size of your ministry, building the kind of environment where people are sought out is a fundamental priority. Success in evangelism depends on it. Faithfulness, in terms of obedience, rides on it as well.

A THREAD YOU CANNOT DENY

Let's return to the ultimate statement of ministry purpose: the Great Commission. One of the major attributes of this command is that Jesus makes clear His assumption that we are already going. The command to make disciples is prefaced with a statement that literally says, "As you are going, make disciples of all nations." Those words summarized what Jesus had been doing all along. Having spent His three years of ministry demonstrating an aggressive relational ministry, Jesus expected His followers to do the same. He has not given us the option to not be aggressive in seeking people.

Christianity is going to people, not asking them to come to us. Real Christianity says, "God so loved He gave," not, "God so loved He waited." When we adopt a posture that requires people to come to us, we send a subtle message of aloofness or spiritual pride. Certainly it is unintentional, but it is not communicating that Christ is willing and able to meet individuals where they are. Jesus made the point loud and clear that the gospel was for all who would receive it. He drove that point home by spending His time with every manner of person from every strata of life.

Building a relational ministry means aggressively seeking those people to whom we want to minister. Jesus' pattern and instructions for ministry billboard this priority. Our faithfulness in following His example is directly related to our effectiveness in carrying out His ministry. This impacts our effectiveness in evangelism. And it applies equally to the equipping aspect of the discipling process.

THE FLIP SIDE OF THE COIN

Lest we get lost among the trees and lose sight of the forest, it is time to rewind our mental tape back to the discussion of chapter 1—our purpose. The premise of this book is that regardless of where a person is spiritually, our challenge is to help him or her follow Christ. We must meet people where they are, not where we want them to be. A disciple-making ministry is one which is able to minister to people at all levels of spiritual maturity and help them follow Christ more completely and more consistently. Settling for an evangelistic or equipping ministry to the essential neglect of the other is unacceptable in light of the Great Commission. We do not have the option to choose either/or.

Thus far this chapter has placed a heavy emphasis on the importance of an intentionally relational ministry as it relates to evangelism. But this kind of ministry is just as important in equipping and nurturing believers. The same practices that fuel evangelism are essential for ministering within the Body. People grow in the context of relationships. They respond to an environment that cares about them. They open up to those who reach out to them.

It has been said that 90 percent of all disciple making is building relationships. Discipling is not a magic curriculum. It is not a seminar. It cannot be accomplished by plugging people into a one-for-all, all-for-one formula. Growing as a disciple of Jesus Christ is a matter of life change, and that kind of change happens in the context of relationships.

Seminaries used to train their students to go regularly on "visitation." It is not uncommon to find pastors who devote an evening a week or a few evenings a month to this practice. As low tech as it may sound, the idea of visitation had its finger directly upon the pulse of this ministry priority. Something happens when those in leadership make contact with their people outside the walls of the church building. Something happens to the pastor or leader, and something happens in the people when they spend time together. Ministry comes to life in relationships, not in the conference room.

It would not be surprising if your internal defenses were up right now. If thoughts of "impracticality" are flashing across your mind, hold on for a minute. Don't write off this principle because your schedule won't allow for another activity each week. The classic practice of "pastoral visitation" is not the only way to make contact with your people. There are many ways to reach out to them and build relationships with them. Let's take this one step at a time.

KEEPING IN TOUCH

You probably have a tremendous desire to make an impact in the lives of your people. Whether you work with students, couples, families, singles, or seniors you are anxious to affect lives with the good news of the gospel. You want your ministry to have profound personal impact. Building a ministry that is able to meet people wherever they are is extremely important.

All of this begs some fundamental questions. If you are going to meet people at their point of need, how can you know where those points of need are? When you teach or preach, how can you be sure your messages are getting through? How can you plan the application of your messages so that they are specifically appropriate for your people? After all, aren't there too many people and too many needs?

Again, the key is to build relationships with people. By regularly making contact with people and spending time with them you will discover where they are. You will be able to learn what needs are present. You will be able to keep in touch. You will be able to accurately evaluate your effectiveness. In short, you will find it much easier to personalize everything you do.

Keeping in touch with people will help you do a better job of guiding your ministry, but it will also yield fruit in the lives of your people. We live in such an impersonal generation that every one of us suffers from feeling that we are just another number. We feel depersonalized by massive bureaucracies. We feel taken advantage of by every sales organization with an auto-dialer. And we feel left alone when it comes to the really important issues of life. Many are afraid that they don't matter that much to anyone at church either.

Leaders in ministry have the power to provide a place where individuals do matter. When you go out of your way to contact people, they realize that they are important—not just another dollar in the offering plate. When you expend your greatest resource—time—contacting people, you are making a priceless investment in your ministry to them.

Iron Sharpens Iron

People grow in relationships. In a relationship where there is trust, there can be vulnerability. There can be a willingness to admit need and to explore change. There can be the support and follow through needed to sustain growth. So the writer of Hebrews urges us to "spur one another on toward love and good deeds" (10:24). God understands the impact one person can have upon another. He made that point a long time ago. In Proverbs He wrote the book on the role of relationships in personal growth. "As iron sharpens iron, so one man sharpens another" (27:17). Without contact there can be no sharpening.

Who has had the greatest spiritual impact on your life? Think about the time that you spent with that person. Think about the things you did. Perhaps it was a college professor, a youth pastor, a friend, your spouse, your parents. Regardless of who it was, you had a relationship with that person. You knew that he or she cared about you. You probably spent time together. You gave him permission, formally or informally, to check up on you. Of all you did together, the key to his influence was probably the way he shared his life with you.

For those people whom you serve, the principle is the same. Offering them quality teaching and personal spiritual integrity is important. And knowing how to be a leader and manager of others helps. But sharing your life with people is the one indispensable gift you can offer. Something unique happens when you are with people outside the walls of your church. When you are on their turf and they are able to see in you a living genuine faith, the dichotomy between organized religion and personal faith is dissolved.

This does not mean you must do everything single-handedly. In fact, the opposite is true. This chapter has stressed the need to permeate your ministry with a relational approach. That means all who are in leadership need to have ownership in this priority. They need to believe in the need and share in the effort. The more people get involved in contacting and relationship building, the more you multiply the depth of your impact.

BACK TO THE TIME CRUNCH

Inertia. Procrastination. Inconvenience. Label it what you like, but the problem is still the same: getting started. Our need is to get started. We need to take the ideas off these pages and weave them into our schedules.

Our schedules! That is where the real crunch is, isn't it? No matter that we deeply desire an intensely relational ministry, it demands *time*. And time is our most precious commodity. We are conditioned to resist anything new or extra that makes a claim upon our time. We already have too many demands clamoring for our time and attention.

Granted, there is no way to escape the fact that a relational ministry will take time. To deny that reality would be dishonest. Perhaps the real need at this point is to help you maximize the efforts you do have time to make. Sometimes having an arsenal of ideas is the best way to overcome the barrier of time pressure. When one idea is inappropriate, another might just fit the bill. To get you started here are a number of ways to make meaningful contact with your people.

DIVIDE AND CONQUER

You are not in this process alone. God has called those who lead the Body of Christ to function as a team, and a relational ministry is not an exception. Share the need with your leadership. Give them a chance to join you in this ministry. You will multiply your impact as you multiply the number of people building bridges to others.

USE "LOBBY TIME"

This may sound so simple that it seems insignificant. Before and after services, meetings, and Bible studies devote your time to meaningful contact and conversation with people. These minutes are usually available in your schedule already. However, it means you cannot use them for last minute prepa-

ration or "official business." Do those things at other times.
Arrive early to get things set up. Don't do cleanup immediately.
Or perhaps recruit others to help with setup and cleanup. Discipline yourself and your leaders to save business discussions for
later so that you might devote this time to others.

THE PHONE

AT&T commercials say, "Long distance, it's the next
best thing to being there," and they're right. The phone is one
of the most convenient ways to "reach out and touch someone." Sometimes when your schedule is tight, a phone call can
accomplish a great deal. It will never replace in-person contact,
but it can supplement other efforts. A call just to touch base and
say hello can be significant.

THE MAILBOX

Make it a habit to write personal notes to people. Our
mailboxes are increasingly filled with impersonal junk mail, so a
handwritten note stands out. It does not have to be long or
elaborate. But written notes convey to people that you care
about them and are thinking about them. In a memorable and
tangible way notes and letters reinforce your other efforts.

PERSONAL CRISES

Personal crises usually demand our attention and call for
involvement. Don't underestimate the power of your presence
with a person during a crisis. When those outside the body hurt
and you are willing to get involved, doors of ministry open.
Your words of concern take on substance, and the love and
stability of Christ can be seen.

MUTUAL INTERESTS

What do you like to do in your spare time? Play golf? Fish?
Hunt? Shop? Work on your car? Are you a garage sale nut?

Without a doubt there are people in your ministry and non-Christians in your sphere of influence who enjoy the same thing. Why not double your efforts? Seek those people, and involve them with you. The times you share together will build a common bond between you. You may even find a new partner for your favorite endeavors.

YOUR OWN AREAS OF NEED

Have you learned the value of being in need? At times we tell ourselves that we need to be in control; we have to be the person who always has something to give. Yet those times when we need assistance from others are often the times we become the most human. Do you need a hand working on your car? Perhaps there are repairs needed on your home. Do you have a hobby or other project that demands greater expertise? Each of these needs can be a perfect time to invite someone else into your life. They might be natural methods for building bridges with non-Christian neighbors and friends. Give others the chance to be the expert in your life. Let them see your humanness through your needs.

GET ON THEIR TURF

All too often we ask people to come to our world, where we have control. Get out of your office and off of your chair, and go visit people where they work and live. At work you might get the chance to meet some of the influential people in their daily lives. You might gain a better understanding of the pressures they face. You may find that a lunch appointment at their office provides a refreshing break for them and meaningful insight for you. At their home you are able to enter the world where they are king, where their lives and roots go deep.

TAKE THE SCALPEL TO YOUR SCHEDULE

Although this is not another idea per se, it is an honest admission. Sooner or later you will need to conduct surgery on your schedule. If building a relationally based ministry is going to be a priority, making time to do something about it is a necessity. Surgery hurts. It always does. But afterward it yields fresh health.

An appropriate place to end this chapter is with this challenge to deal with your schedule. Why not take the time right now to look it over carefully. Candidly evaluate the activities that are crowding out your time for people. You might find that things cannot be changed until a creative solution is discovered. Or, you might find that those things that have eaten up your time are merely optional endeavors that have slowly and silently crowded out the essentials.

Acts 6 tells us that the apostles had run into a crucial time crunch problem. They were forced to evaluate the cause and then devise a creative solution. Their time was being consumed by waiting on tables. Where is yours going? Involve others who know you in the evaluation and the solution process of carving out the time you need. Invite others to hold you accountable so that your problem does not become one of procrastination as well.

7

COMMUNICATING
CHRIST CLEARLY

*I, when I am lifted up . . . , will draw all
men to myself.*

—John 12:32

Let's assume for the moment that you have successfully
woven the first two foundational practices into the life of
your congregation. Your people love and are loved. Relationships have never been stronger. And you have personally done
so much contacting that they are sick of seeing your face. Now
what?

As we look back to the life of Christ, it is clear that Jesus
faced a generation that was looking for a triumphant political
savior. They wanted a powerful king riding a white horse, but
He came as a suffering servant astride an awkward donkey. He
simply didn't fit the mold that had been publicly predetermined
for Him. Yet a right relationship with Him could only be based
on accurate knowledge of who He was. This need was so great
that much of His early ministry was specifically devoted to helping His disciples understand His identity. In fact, throughout
the course of His entire ministry He never ceased working on
this issue.

Misconceptions and disinformation about the Person, the
work, and the message of Christ abound in our day as well. In

fact, in many ways, popular thinking about Jesus today is so inadequate that we face an uphill challenge as great or greater than the one He faced. At times you might feel like salmon swimming upstream as you try to set the record straight.

A third priority for building an environment that nurtures growth is to communicate a clear understanding of Christ. Help people understand who Christ really is. Clear up misconceptions and false ideas about the identity and message of Christ. Our task is not so different from that of Christ Himself.

We live among a generation of skeptics. Jesus' claim that He is the only way to salvation doesn't sell well on Broadway. His deity, His birth, His miracles—almost every aspect of His life has come under question. But even more significant, there is an absence of accurate knowledge about Christ among the general public. We can no longer assume a degree of spiritual understanding by the world. This biblical vacuum necessitates that we become relentless in our attempts to help people know and understand Christ.

The salmon provides a good parallel to the task before us. When the time comes for a salmon to spawn, she leaves the cold turbulent waters of the Pacific and travels upstream, heading for calm headwaters where she might lay her eggs. However, the journey is neither calm nor peaceful. The salmon must literally jump over rocks and climb waterfalls. From a human standpoint the journey appears majestic. In many places you can see fish jumping and straining against the current. These beautiful, powerful fish single-mindedly pursue their goal, in spite of the cost, unwilling to turn back for any reason.

Communicating a proper understanding of Christ may feel like trying to swim upstream against an inexhaustible force. But we have no option. It is difficult, maybe even impossible, for a person to yield his life to Someone he does not know. Right motivations for service and ministry only stem from a right understanding of Christ. Those who experience new birth in Christ have a great need to learn of Him. Those who are al-

ready Christians need to be continually reminded of who He is
and what He said. As we know Him we are drawn to Him. As
we are drawn to Him we are eager to please Him.

LEADERS ALWAYS GO FIRST

Without doubt you already share our conviction of the importance of knowing Christ and making Him known. You are
committed to helping your people develop an accurate understanding of who He is. Yet experience shows that sometimes
even the strongest intentions can be subtly diluted or even di-
verted entirely. The result? Good intentions cease to become
anything more than just intentions.

This book is not about intentions. It is about action and
change whenever necessary. However, action and change begin
first and foremost in the life of the one who leads. The modeling
process is unavoidable. If Christ is not being clearly understood
by those in our ministries, we cannot pass the buck. We cannot
look elsewhere. We must first look at our own lives. How well
do we know Christ? How aggressively do we personally pursue
a greater understanding of our Savior? Our own understanding
of Jesus Christ is perhaps the most influential factor in our ability to shape other people's concept of Christ.

You see, if this priority is not really part of your own life,
it will never become an authentic priority in your ministry. Unless it is a deep personal conviction, we will give lip service to
this need, but other things will continually preempt our plans to
pursue it. Authentic ministry begins when leaders bring themselves under the searchlight of God's Spirit and cry, "Lord begin Your work with me."

Helping your people develop a healthy understanding of
our Savior begins when you work to insure that your own understanding of Christ is clear. It begins when those who lead
recognize that as Paul said, "You are a letter from Christ" (2
Cor. 3:3*a*). Our passion to know Jesus Christ will be read by
those we serve. Our own understanding of Christ will also give

us the personal impetus to carry out specific efforts to make Him known.

STUDY YOUR CULTURE

Some people, because of their own personal background, misunderstand the message of Christ entirely. Others have serious barriers against God because of the relationship they had with their own father. In different parts of the country and in different subcultures within society you can find different factors influencing people's understanding of Christ. Your challenge as a shepherd of the Body is to discover these false ideas about Christ. Knowing where your people are is a major step in helping them discover the real person, work, and message of Christ.

Your study of your culture can be done using simple communication tools.

Observing: Watch how people discuss Christ or react to discussion about Him. Are they ashamed of Him? Do they shrink at the mention of His name from fear? Using your senses can tell you a great deal.

Listening: Listen with a discerning ear to conversations about Christ. What is missing? What is overemphasized? What is simply stated improperly?

Questioning: Ask questions in a creative manner to determine ideas and opinions that people have. This approach might supply just the insight you need. Try questions like these: "If Jesus would come back today, what kind of occupation do you think He would have? What kind of message would He have for the church in our day?" Or try this one, "If you could ask Jesus any question at all, what would you ask Him?"

Just as missionaries who want to reach different people groups with the gospel must first study their culture, so we need to be students of our own culture. The more we understand where people are, the more we can target our efforts for maximum impact. Few things are more enjoyable in ministry than bringing Christ out of history and into the present for people.

EVALUATE YOUR TEACHING EMPHASIS

When we teach, what do we emphasize? Do we emphasize what to do for God, or do we emphasize who God is and what He has done for us? Only the second emphasis places a priority on communicating Christ clearly.

Richard Howard in his book *Newness of Life* states that the pattern of Scripture, and especially Paul's writing, is first and foremost an emphasis upon who God is and what He has done for us. Only when we begin to learn those two things do we truly serve Him for proper reasons. Our doing is in response to His being.

Only after articulating facts of God's character and work does Paul talk about what we should be doing. You can observe this in the way Paul uses the imperative tense—the tense of command—in the second part of his letters. Take a look at the book of Romans, for example. In Romans you see the shift in focus at the beginning of chapter 12: "Therefore, I urge you brothers, in view of God's mercy. . . . " God's mercies had been laid out in chapters 1-11.

To make clear this biblical pattern, a few more examples might be helpful. One brief but powerful example was when God called Isaiah to be His spokesman. God could have commanded him directly or laid out a propositional argument. But Isaiah 6 begins with a vision of God giving Isaiah a glimpse of what God is like. Another example is the book of Ephesians, which can be divided right down the middle. Chapters 1-3 talk about all that God has done for us, and then chapters 4-6 detail implications for our behavior. One other example can be found in Lewis Sperry Chafer's study of thirty-three things that God does for every believer at the moment of salvation. Thirty-three things![1] Before we have a chance to begin doing anything for God, He has already done an overwhelming amount of work on our behalf.

It is easy to lose this emphasis. If you are regularly in a teaching role, try teaching without using words such as *should, ought,* or *do.* If your responsibilities do not normally include teaching, try another experiment. At your next study of any kind take a piece of scratch paper and count the number of times statements are made about what you should be doing.

In our zeal for growth and spiritual effectiveness it is very easy to overemphasize what people should be doing for Christ. However, a proper understanding of Him is the key to rightly motivated obedience and service. Lift Him up consistently and clearly before your people. He will draw all men to Himself.

Get Beyond the Dust of History

The challenge of communicating a healthy understanding of Christ is acute. It means helping people relate to a living Savior whom they cannot see. Unfortunately, it is easy to view the Bible as ancient history. Because the trappings of the gospel existed in Middle Eastern antiquity, it can be difficult for people to understand how Jesus relates to their lives in a high tech era—hence one of the greatest challenges for the teacher or preacher of the gospel.

How can we intentionally bring those elements of history alive today? One of the best guidelines can be clearly stated in a single sentence. *Put yourself in the shoes of people who were there!*

Jesus spent His life interacting with people. Every person watching, listening, being healed, or standing in His presence for even a moment was someone like us. They had questions, concerns, and needs like ours. Putting yourself into their shoes sheds new light on the dynamics of what took place. As a result, those to whom you minister will be better able to understand and relate to the ministry of Jesus.

A fascinating exercise to help you do this is to use your senses. How did things look? What would you have seen people doing if you had been there? Were there any interesting sounds? What conversations might have taken place between others in the crowd? What time of day was it, and did the weather have any effect on the atmosphere? Were there any smells that might have colored the experience?

Perhaps an actual example might help. You know the events of the hallelujah parade on that first Palm Sunday. But have you ever thought about it in terms of what it must have been like for the people who were there? Jesus of Nazareth was riding an awkward, never-before-ridden donkey. And there were hordes of people laying their cloaks down before Him in an impromptu red carpet. Is there any chance that the nervous beast of burden suffered from a weak bladder that day? If so, you saw the effects of that nervous tension right before your eyes. Now Jesus has almost reached you. Will you lay your cloak down for him? The cloak you wear is your only outer garment, and if anything happens to it what will you do? Thus the significance of what each person did to honor Christ with his or her clothing that day comes to life.

When the parade reached the peak of the Mount of Olives, imagine the sounds. As the crowd sang and shouted their hosannas, their praise must have carried across the valley below and echoed back off the walls of the city. They were in an instant symphony of echoing praise that must have filled the air with electric excitement. Jesus' words about the stones crying out might very well have been in reference to the stones of the city walls. At that very moment those stones were echoing praise back to the crowd on the hill.

Sensory experiences are memorable and moving. Bringing them to life can help people connect with a situation from long ago. As a result, the gap of two thousand years closes quickly.

Getting beyond the sense of the Bible and the ministry of Christ as history alone is a profoundly significant way to help people understand Christ. When we see Jesus relating to people who experienced the same feelings we have, His ministry comes to life for us. We learn to understand the eternal relevance of His words. This demands work and time, but it is rewarding. It makes a lasting difference, tangibly helping people follow Christ more consistently and completely.

Note

1. Lewis Sperry Chafer, *Systematic Theology,* vol. 3 (Dallas: Dallas Seminary, 1948), pp. 234-65.

8

A HEALTHY GROUP IMAGE

Every group, every club, every church, and every ministry has an image of itself. In fact, every person within a group has his or her own version of that image. You and your church are no exception. Stop for a moment—what are the first thoughts that come to your mind when you think of your church or ministry? Those thoughts are a part of your group image. That image may be positive, exciting, frustrating, depressing, or anything in between.

A healthy group image is directly connected to our effectiveness in helping people grow as disciples of Christ. It is a major part of a nurturing environment. Therefore leaders in the church of Jesus Christ have the responsibility to create and nourish a healthy group image among those to whom we minister. We need to recognize that our group image will either contribute to or hinder the impact of our ministry.

A HEALTHY GROUP IMAGE IN ACTION

Under the inspiration of the Holy Spirit, Luke recorded the events of the early church. In so doing he also gave us insights into the dynamics at work behind those historic events. Acts 2:42-47 has long been recognized as a summary statement of life in the early church. Have you ever noticed the clues in those verses about the healthy group image present there? We

see at least four insights into the image the early Christians
held of that church.

1. THEY WERE DEVOTED (v. 42)

The people were devoted and committed to one another
as well as to the ministry and mission of the church. Literally
you could say that they had bound their hearts together for the
duration. It was long-term devotion. Needless to say, that level
of commitment happens in direct proportion to a general enthusiasm for the cause.

2. THEY WERE TOGETHER WITH ONENESS (vv. 44, 46)

Their spiritual unity was demonstrated by the way they
were continually meeting together. People who are not enthusiastic about a group do not frequently go out of their way to
participate in it. Yet those early Christians met together daily in
the Temple, in their homes, for study and for meals. They were
inseparable.

3. THERE WAS A SENSE OF GLADNESS (vv. 46-47)

Luke tells us that there was an overwhelmingly positive
attitude among these believers. Sincere gladness and praise
flowed freely whenever they gathered together.

4. THEY ENJOYED THE FAVOR OF ALL THE PEOPLE (v. 47)

Perhaps most instructive of all is this final phrase. The
image of this early church was so healthy that it made an impact
on those outside the church.

THE IMPACT OF A HEALTHY GROUP IMAGE

Some will react to this idea of building a healthy group
image with skepticism. "Just preach the Word," they might
say. Preaching the Word is foundational, but it is not the only

task of leaders in the church of Christ. The early church had an explosive impact on the world, and Acts 2 demonstrates the link between the healthy dynamics of that body and its impact. In our own ministries, the impact of our group image will be felt in at least three other crucial areas.

TEACHABILITY

Stated in the first person, this principle is: "The more excited I am about the group, the more receptive I am to the things I learn there." You have probably witnessed the truth of this principle borne out when members of your church attend a retreat or seminar. They leave with a great attitude and come back raving about the profound influence it made on their lives.

Em Griffin, a professor of communications and a specialist on the implications for Christian ministry, has done much research on this subject. From his study he has discovered that when you increase the health of a group's self-image the people of that group become more eager, receptive, and responsive as learners.[1]

On the contrary, when people hold a low view of their group they hold a low view of the things taught there. The higher the group image the more open people are to the teaching. You can see this when people come expecting significant results from services and Bible studies. A healthy group image changes the way people feel about being there. And naturally, if people are eager to participate, they are more enthused about inviting others.

OUTREACH ORIENTATION

The higher the image people in your ministry have of your church, the more willing they will be to bring others. Conversely, the lower their image of the group, the greater their resistance to reaching out to others.

It makes sense. When a person regards something highly, he is proud to belong and comfortable recommending it to a friend. However, when he is uncertain or negative about the ministry, he won't recommend it for fear of being embarrassed and ashamed. It is possible that a poor group image is a major barrier to outreach in many churches. The people in your church will be open to bringing others in direct proportion to their level of enthusiasm toward the church and its ministries.

COMMITMENT TO THE CAUSE

In addition to the impact on teachability and outreach orientation, a healthy group image has a direct bearing on the level of tangible commitment. Commitment is often expressed in our usual list of stewardship issues. How often do urgent needs for workers and finances arise? And how often are these needs publicly discussed in guilt-laden tones? Such unmet needs are possibly the result of a poor group image. Furthermore, the hammer of guilt will only compound the problem if a poor group image is responsible for the problem.

When people believe in the ministry, their tangible commitment will follow naturally. That commitment is often demonstrated by increased giving and greater personal involvement.

You may or may not have wrestled with the importance of a healthy group image before. However, you have surely spent time working to create the results that it brings. Building a healthy group image must be an ongoing focus. It is one of those six fundamental priorities essential for a discipling environment. It too begins in the life of the leader. Addressing this need means beginning with your own life.

You Cannot Not Communicate

Researchers in the field of communication have long discussed the fact that more than 50 percent of the messages we send are communicated nonverbally. Body language and tone of voice communicate more than words. That means the things you feel are observed by others, regardless of what you say or do not say. People read your nonverbal language; hence you cannot *not* communicate.

Call it self-fulfilling prophecy, or anything you like, but over the course of time the group image of your ministry will reflect your own attitudes. Encouraging? Scary? Frustrating? Be honest with yourself, and evaluate the image you have of your group. To ignore how you truly feel is to ignore the reality of what you communicate. In fact, if you find yourself frustrated and down on your people they probably sense it and are, as they say on the beach, "bummed out."

No one would dare say that changing your attitude is easy. Doing so is accomplished much as any other internal change. You begin at the fountain of new life—on your knees. Pour your heart out to the Lord, and ask Him to bring about the growth and change you need. Turn your need over to the Father who gives to all men generously. Ask Him to give you a new perspective on the people and the ministry to which He has called you. Seek the sustaining and transforming work of His hand to nourish a healthy image of your ministry.

In addition to honest personal evaluation and accompanying efforts to improve your own attitude, making a few important actions regular habits will serve you well. The three practices that follow are powerful tools for encouraging a healthy outlook. In many ways they will put feet to your prayers. They will make a noticeable difference in your people and in your own life.

Parade the Potential, Not the Problems

Scripture is filled with examples of people who had reasons to be discouraged but were not consumed by them. When confronted by problems they focused on the potential. In spite of drastic situations, they identified assurances of hope. If we do the same, our own perspective will be elevated to greater health. And as we do so, the health of our group's image will grow dramatically too.

Paul's letters to the Christians in Corinth make clear that that church had more than its share of troubles. There were factions, confusions, sinful behavior, and more. Yet he still found reason to praise them. He elevated their potential, not the problems: "I always thank God for you because of his grace given you in Christ Jesus. For in him you have been enriched in every way. . . . I praise you for remembering me in everything and for holding to the teachings, just as I passed them on to you" (1 Cor. 1:4; 11:2).

When Moses sent the spies to check out the Promised Land, Joshua and Caleb saw the same sights as the other ten spies. They saw the obstacles, and they felt the sway of public opinion back home. Yet they publicly defended a different perspective. Why? What had they seen differently? While the ten were noticing how big the sons of Anak were, Joshua and Caleb were remembering how big their God was. When the ten saw the fortified cities, Joshua and Caleb saw the fruit of the land. When the ten were scared off by cities high in the hills, the two were encouraged by their God who reigns high in the heavens. When the nation was afraid that they were too weak to proceed, Joshua and Caleb had faith in God's strength.[2] For them, it was a matter of perspective and faith.

A classic story has been told about two young boys who were identical twins. From birth they were impossible to tell apart, except for one feature. One boy was always negative whereas the other was always positive. Regardless of the circumstances, this trait always held true. One boy would always be down and depressed, but his twin was always up.

Teachers and counselors in school were more than a little puzzled by this glaring dissimilarity. As a result the boys were taken through a series of psychological tests. In one test the two boys were put into separate identical rooms full of the newest and best toys on the market, where they could play alone. After a period of time the researchers reentered the room to see how the boys were getting along. Their discoveries were predictable.

The usually negative boy was having a horrible time. They found him sitting in the corner moaning about toys that weren't there and crying over toys he couldn't get to work right. Meanwhile, the second boy was having the time of his life in the other room. They found him trying to play with as many toys as possible—simultaneously.

The doctors were baffled and decided to try something a bit out of the ordinary. They took the generally happy boy and placed him in a room devoid of everything but a large pile of manure heaped up in the center of the floor. After telling him to wait for them there, the researchers left the room. Within a matter of moments everyone heard the boy whooping and hollering at the top of his lungs. Afraid something might be wrong, they all rushed back to see what was the matter.

What did they find? The boy was on top of the manure pile scooping up handfuls and throwing it everywhere. In spite of the odor, he was in boyish ecstasy having the time of his life. The doctors probed the boy with obvious questions. "Son, what on earth are you so excited about?" The boy answered, "With all this manure, there has to be a pony in here somewhere!"

Leaders can help people discover that obstacles are opportunities for faith. It is a matter of perspective. Sometimes you need to help them look for the pony. You can help them find reasons for encouragement in the midst of circumstances that appear discouraging. Or you can allow them to become buried under potential problems lurking in the future. Focus continually on the things that are wrong, and your group image will be destroyed. Focus on what God can do in your circumstances, and an attitude of expectancy will be cultivated in your ministry.

Do not misunderstand. The message here is not that we should become cheerleaders of mindless enthusiasm. God has called us to a work of substance. He has called us to the most ambitious effort on the face of the globe—the effort to redeem every man and woman from the plague and penalty of sin. Precisely because this is His work and because the gates of hell will not prevail against it, we have reason to be enthusiastic.

CLARIFY AND COMMUNICATE VISION

A healthy group image is not just a collective experience of "warm fuzzies." Rather, it is a tangible enthusiasm about the work God is currently doing and the work He wants to do in the future. Just as the word *enthusiasm* literally means, "God in us," a healthy group image is built upon His active presence.

Developing the ability to verbalize vision—that purpose or driving passion God has given you for your ministry—can be a powerful tool. A clearly communicated vision connects purpose with conviction, provides substance to enthusiasm, and fuels godly dreaming—all of which contribute to a healthy group image.

What has God called you and your church to do? Can you crystallize it into a memorable sentence? Put it in words so that it might be communicated. The more transferable the better. By clarifying and communicating the vision God has given you, you give people a rallying cry. You help them take ownership in the fact that God has called you together for a specific purpose.

Jesus cultivated and confirmed His vision for His disciples in many ways. The Great Commission expressed it most succinctly, but all along the way He had set the stage. Listen to the following examples, and consider what an impact they must have made on the disciples.

> Come follow me . . . and I will make you fishers of men. (Matt. 4:19)
>
> On this rock I will build my church, and the gates of Hades will not overcome it. (Matt. 16:18)
>
> I tell you the truth, anyone who has faith in me will do what I have been doing. He will do even greater things than these, because I am going to the Father. (John 14:12)
>
> You will receive power when the Holy Spirit comes on you; and you will be my witnesses in Jerusalem, and in all Judea and Samaria, and to the ends of the earth. (Acts 1:8)

From His initial invitation until His final words to them, Jesus communicated to His disciples that He had great plans for their lives. He had dreams and purpose for them. He believed in—He counted on—the potential of their ministry.

But many churches have such a watered-down, generic sense of purpose, it's no wonder people aren't excited. In many cases asking leaders what vision they have for their ministry would produce embarrassed babbling. They would likely hem and haw, grasping for biblical sounding words. In some cases, the vision some hold for their ministries is nothing more than the vague notion of being "the church." For example, "Our church exists to be a church!"

Later in this book (chap. 17), we will discuss a practical method for clarifying personal vision. For now, begin to let the pot simmer on this question of vision. Growing a healthy group image is one major benefactor of clear vision.

CELEBRATE THE WAY GOD HAS WORKED

One final thought about building a healthy group image: celebrate the good times! This is one of the simplest and most easily workable ideas. Whenever something good happens in your congregation, review it publicly with the whole body.

Most of us have selective memory. We remember in detail those things which went wrong, and we forget the details about the things that went well. Reviewing the good times can help counteract this tendency. Remembering is so important in Scripture that a theology of remembrance could easily be constructed. Over and over again God tells His people to remember what He has done and how far they have come. Elaborate memorials were constructed. Many of the feasts are designed specifically to assist the remembering process.

Biblically speaking, God's desire is to provoke healthy remembrance of the good times in general and His works in specific. In Psalm 78, God makes clear that the Israelites lost perspective spiritually because they did not remember His works. "They forgot what he had done, the wonders he had shown them" (v. 11).

The group image in your ministry might well be suffering from selective memory. Perhaps the lack of enthusiasm has been created by a forgetfulness about God's work in the past. By helping people remember, you follow God's prescription. You also create momentum for renewed vigor. Therefore, celebrate—continually review—the good times in any and every way possible.

Think about the normal vehicles of communication used in your ministry. A weekly bulletin? Monthly newsletter? Periodic mailings? Bulletin boards? Special reports in certain services? Annual reports? Congregational meetings? Every one of those items can be an ideal opportunity for reviewing the progress and positive events within your body. Each one is already in place and would require no extra work—just a different focus.

If you are like many ministries, you experience weekly or monthly pressure to write an interesting newsletter. You know how important good communication is, but the regular grind of cranking out these pieces gets old. Celebrating God's work in the body may be your answer. In place of filling page after page with announcements, review the good times. Publicly replay the ways God has worked. Communicate answers to prayer, conversions to Christ, progress on church goals, spiritual milestones (personal or corporate), and even financial blessings.

At this point some people in difficult circumstances might be tempted to cry, "How can we celebrate the way God has been working when God is not working in our church!" Even in the most trying situations, leadership's task is to discern how God is working. It is certain that He is at work, for if God were not working He would be dead.

A healthy group image will affect every area of your ministry. In one sense it will feed everything you do. In another sense it will be fed by everything you do. Like most priorities, making it happen is a burden that comes with the mantle of leadership. But building a healthy group image can be one of the most enjoyable tasks of leadership. Everyone likes to be the bearer of good news!

Notes

1. Em Griffen, *The Mindchangers* (Wheaton, Ill.: Tyndale, 1976), p. 202. See also sections titled "Mold," chaps. 8-11.

2. See Numbers 13 to observe how the issue was a matter of perspective, not certain disaster.

9

A PRAYER BASE

The kingdom of God does not consist in words, but in power.

—1 Cor. 4:20, NASB

The sheer magnitude of the idea that we can communicate directly with God stirs our souls. Its potential impact enthralls our minds. And volumes of discussion on it occupy our bookshelves.

It is natural that the more deeply something touches people the more frequently it is written about. And prayer demonstrates this truth. In fact, so much has been said about the practice, potential, and priority of prayer that this chapter might be the most dangerous of the entire book—not because some wild new insight will be unraveled but because it could contribute to a vicarious satisfaction with prayer.

You see, it is easy to feel a superficial satisfaction when discussing prayer without actually praying. We can listen to another person's experience and feel encouraged or uplifted. We can read or study about prayer and think that knowing more puts us in better stead. But prayer is participation, not a spectator sport. Studying and growing in our understanding of prayer can be beneficial, but only as that knowledge is applied in practice. When it is not applied, more information only serves to numb our sense of need.

Yet we have no choice. If we are going to pattern our ministries after that of the Master, we must examine our practice of prayer. Mobilizing a prayer base that bathes our ministries and people in prayer is undeniably a foundational priority. Drop your personal defenses or feelings of overfamiliarity that might keep you from honest assessment. Read these pages with a teachable heart. Ask the Holy Spirit to speak to you about the health of the prayer base in your ministry. As you read this chapter, expect Him to give you ideas and insights perfectly in tune with the needs and opportunities before you.

Seek the Hand of God

Imagine being forced to judge the secrets of life-changing ministry by the contents of your mailbox. You would probably decide that life-changing ministry is the result of discovering the right program. Based on the mail we receive, it would be easy to assume that there is a magic curriculum, a perfect program out there that does the job. Direct mail is aimed at our predisposition to rely on programs, to rely on our fondness for the tangible things we can do. Most of us have a tendency to believe we have the ability to accomplish spiritual results. It seems that we have missed the point of 1 Corinthians 4:20: "The kingdom of God does not consist in words, but in power" (NASB).

The kingdom of God is not defined by programs, curriculum, video libraries, creative clip-art, or any other ministry tool. The kingdom—God's rule and reign in the lives of His people—is a matter of spiritual power. God's work in people's lives is not merely enhanced human endeavor. It is the supernatural work of a supernatural God invading the natural world of our lives.

If those of us who have been called to be leaders in the Body of Christ do not come to grips with our need to pray, we will not see the fruit of changed lives. If we allow ourselves to fall prey to the temptation of trying to do in the flesh what only God can do by the Spirit, we are doomed. It is time to seek the hand of God in our ministries and in the lives of our people. Because we desire to see God do His kind of work, we must work according to His method. Prayer is that method.

Jacob is well known as a schemer. Repeatedly he chose to use human means, crafty ones at that, to accomplish what he was afraid God could not do alone. Finally he met his match. As he was returning to the land of his family, he heard the news that Esau was coming. Esau, the brother whom he had cheated, was coming to meet him. Esau, the mighty hunter, was coming with four hundred men. Not surprisingly, Jacob was filled with "great fear and distress" (Gen. 32:6-7).

Forced by fear to face his need, Jacob then turned to prayer. In fact he spent an entire night alone, much of it devoted to prayer. You know what happened the following night. God appeared to him as a man and proceeded to wrestle with Jacob. Jacob was so intent on receiving God's blessing that he wrestled with God all night long.

Throughout the Scriptures there are accounts of men and women who sought the hand of God in the face of their needs —men and women who would not let go because they knew their only hope lay in the work God could do. For those of us in ministry today, there is no difference. Our only hope lies in the supernatural work that God alone can do. It is time for us to wrestle with God, that He might pour Himself out upon us.

Follow the Example of Christ

If any man ever could have claimed that he didn't need to pray, Jesus was that man. After all, He knew the Father's heart, He knew His mission, He was a master at discerning needs, and He was the second member of the Trinity. Yet He was continually devoting time to prayer.

Mark 1 recounts the activities of Jesus one Sabbath. We discussed this day in the life of Christ in an earlier chapter, but we did not look at what happened the following day. Jesus' Sabbath had been demanding, draining, and just plain long. His ministry to the sick and demon-possessed had continued late into the night. Yet the next morning He did not sleep in. "Very early in the morning, while it was still dark, Jesus got up, left the house and went off to a solitary place, where he prayed" (Mark 1:35). Anyone who serves as a pastor or leader in a church knows how draining a long day of ministry can be. Rising before dawn for the purpose of prayer after one of those long days is possible only when it is a matter of highest priority.

Matthew gives us another glimpse of Jesus' priority to spend time alone in prayer. After hearing the news of John the Baptist's death, Jesus attempted to pull away from the crowds to a solitary place. But the crowds followed Him, so He ministered to them. His ministry that day culminated in the famous story of the miraculous feeding of the five thousand. In spite of the fact that this was the end of a day that included the sad news about John, a trip across the lake, ministry to the sick and needy in an immense crowd, and a rather intense banquet, Jesus' next move was to spend time in prayer. "After he had dismissed [the crowd], he went up on a mountainside by himself to pray" (Matt. 14:23). He stayed there until "the fourth watch of the night" (v. 25), which was at least 3:00 in the morning![1]

One more example should drive the point home permanently. It was time for Jesus to formally appoint those whom He would train to be leaders after Him. We know them as the twelve apostles. Out of the crowds that consistently followed Him, whom would He pick? Many had demonstrated faithfulness to Him and responsiveness to His message, but to whom would He give the keys of the kingdom? Because Jesus was a master at discerning what was in the hearts of men, you might think He would rely on His own wisdom to select these men. But He did not do it without prayer! "One of those days Jesus went out to a mountainside to pray, and spent the night praying to God. When morning came, he called his disciples to him and chose twelve of them, whom he also designated apostles" (Luke 6:12-13).

SIMPLE STRATEGIES WORK BEST

At this point we can summarize all that has been said about prayer this way: Do it! Dive in. Set aside time. Perform surgery on your schedule or on that of your church if you have to. Create a place for prayer, and then pray. You need to make prayer an activity that underlies and permeates every aspect of your ministry.

Many people have worked hard over the years to create methods that assist the process of prayer. The methods that are most helpful tend to be those which are simple. The more simple a tool the better. You see, a simple method fosters prayer, not preparation. The more complicated or time-consuming the method, the less actual prayer takes place. Keep things simple, and you will involve the greatest number of people in the greatest amount of actual prayer.

The following methods for encouraging more intelligent and consistent prayer are effective. Perhaps they might stimulate your own ideas for ways to increase the prayer base for your ministry.

PRAYER CHAINS

The prayer chain is an effective way to spread the word about specific needs for prayer. This method is a must-have. Over time, however, you might find it helpful to reacquaint every member of the prayer chain with specific instructions for keeping the requests accurate and moving and keeping the purpose—actual prayer—clear.

PRAYER CALENDARS

One church publishes a monthly prayer calendar that identifies a different family in the church to pray for each day. Obviously not every family is prayed for during the month, but this system has proved to be manageable and easy to use. Some families pray for those listed every morning at breakfast. Others pray for the designated family at dinner time. Still others keep the prayer calendar in their own prayer journal and use it during their daily quiet time.

PRAYER MEETINGS

Have you ever thought about setting aside a special time just for prayer? The old midweek prayer meeting is not what it used to be, but there is great value in meetings devoted to prayer. Committees and leadership boards can benefit greatly from adjusting their agendas so that entire meetings might be devoted to prayer.

CONCERTS OF PRAYER

David Bryant has become the foremost spokesperson for the concert of prayer movement. His writings identify plans to gather groups of all sizes together in order to participate in extended periods of prayer. Whole churches and conferences have used this approach.[2]

SPECIFIC DAYS OF PRAYER AND FASTING

One church regularly designates a day to be set aside for prayer and fasting for a particular area of ministry. Extensive lists of requests, plans, and reports of praise are printed up and distributed. Before and after work, people gather at the church to pray together as they fast through a meal. Those who cannot attend pray at home or during their lunch hour. The printed list of requests is key to helping people participate.

PRAYER JOURNALS OR NOTEBOOKS

Nothing encourages sustained prayer as much as records of God's answers. A prayer notebook is a valid tool for groups just as it is for individuals. Elder boards, deacon boards, church committees, and any other group within the church can find this approach to prayer stimulating and encouraging. Small group bible studies find it especially helpful to keep some form of "answer book" that records the ways God has moved in response to their prayers.

On the Personal Side

In all of this discussion about involving people in prayer, keep in mind one other thought: Prayer is not just something our people need to do. *We* need to pray! We need to become so captivated by the need and potential for prayer that we refuse to allow anything to crowd it out of our lives. We need to wrestle with God, refusing to accept anything less than His work in our midst.

Moses held those convictions. For him communication with the Father was so crucial that he set up a special tent outside the camp where he might go and pray. On a regular basis he would go out to the tent in order to meet with God (see Ex. 33:7-11). If you think that was easy for him, guess again.

Moses may have had the most demanding job of any human being in all of time. His task was to forge a nation out of more than a million refugees foraging their way through the desert. And the people were not exactly the most cooperative. Yet he made it his habit to remain devoted to prayer. He was a man who would settle for nothing less than the supernatural work of God Himself.

One day while speaking to the Lord, Moses prayed a most audacious prayer. Let's eavesdrop on his conversation for a moment. "If your Presence does not go with us, do not send us up from here" (Ex. 33:15). Did you catch that? Moses is telling the Lord that he will stay right there in the desert if the Lord himself does not personally lead them. He was willing to stay in the desert—snakes, heat, complaining, and all! He was willing to give up the land of promise if the God of those promises would not lead the way Himself. There was no substitute.

There was no acceptable alternative. The only hope they had of success was in the active presence of the Lord among them.

Things are no different today. The only hope we have for seeing changed lives is the active work of God among us. Ministry that is successfully reaching people for Christ and helping them follow Him can only happen by His power. Leaders who eagerly desire such a ministry must learn to lead from their knees, with prayers of desperation, just as Moses did. We need to be actively committed to seeking His face in all that we do.

Carl Wilson put it all together when he wrote these words: "Prayer is one of the most important aspects of building disciples. If we are to help people grow in their knowledge of Jesus Christ we must pray. In fact, if we do everything else right, but fail to pray, nothing significant will happen."[3]

Notes

1. The fourth watch would normally have been the last watch of the night, approximately 3:00–6:00 A.M.

2. Information and materials can be obtained through Concerts of Prayer International; Pentagon Towers; P.O. Box 36008; Minneapolis, MN 55435.

3. Carl Wilson, *With Christ in the School of Disciple Building* (Grand Rapids: Zondervan, 1976), p. 223.

10

COMMUNICATING THE WORD

Imagine a typical family on their way home from church. Dad and Mom are in the front seat. Their beautiful children in the backseat peacefully ignore their growling stomachs. Dad asks, "What did you learn in Sunday school today, son?"

The boy looks at his father with a bright smile—obviously excited about the lesson of the day. Dad notices the gleam in the eyes of his budding theologian and waits eagerly for the report. "Well, Dad," the son begins, "my teacher told us the story of the green guy."

"The green guy?" asks Dad, rather puzzled.

"Yeah, there was this one guy traveling along the road when some really bad guys jumped out from somewhere and beat him up. After they stole his money, his credit cards, and his donkey, they left him there on the side of the road. Some other people came along, and no one would help him except for the green guy."

"But, son, who is the green guy?"

"I don't know, Dad. My teacher just picked him up from a stack of other people and put him up on the flannel board."

Have you ever had a conversation like that with your son or daughter? On the one hand it is cute to hear their version of the Bible stories. But on the other hand it's a little scary to think that in spite of our efforts to communicate clearly, kids don't always understand.

However, the Bible contains more than just cute stories. It is the living Word of God. The Scriptures are God's eternally relevant words for every one of us. The Word contains all we need to know to live godly and upright lives. Yet how much do people really know the Word? How well are they able to search it and apply it to their own lives? How many passages do they know well enough to recite by memory or meditate upon through the day? Have the people we serve moved beyond the biblical confusion of "the story of the green guy"?

Recent studies done in evangelical churches have uncovered an alarming rate of biblical illiteracy. If we are to build ministries that enable people to grow in Christ, we must consistently communicate the Word. We must conquer the problem of biblical illiteracy and help people connect their lives to the wisdom of the Scriptures.

You know these things to be true. In fact, you are probably already working to keep the Word open before your people. You have a strong desire for those in your church to discover the life-changing work of the Word in their lives that you have known in your life.

Why then devote an entire chapter to the priority of the Word? The purpose of this chapter is not to convince you of the importance of God's Word. Rather, the need is for you to check your bearings, to make sure that your practice is in line with your priorities. In addition, there is a need to reaffirm and rediscover practical ideas that will bring ongoing health to your efforts to communicate the Word.

WAYS WE GET SIDETRACKED

Like most challenges of leadership, the danger before us is usually not blatantly obvious. Rather, it is typically the subtle problem of slow drift. Over the course of time it is easy to drift one or two degrees, until suddenly you find yourself off course. None of us is immune; the danger is real. Bottom line, the danger is that when we are pulled off course, the Word is not communicated clearly or adequately. Four specific dangers have sidetracked many and taken a great toll on the impact of the Word. Take a good look to see that you have not fallen victim to their lures.

TEACHING ABOUT THE WORD

Even the most diligent teacher or preacher can get caught up talking about the Bible without looking directly into the Bible. It happens even with good curriculum or study guides. In a small group Bible study, good discussion flows out of a focus on the study guide but may ignore the Word you gathered to study. At other times teachers get so wrapped up in the ideas and views of commentators and other authors that they teach on the comments about the Scriptures instead of on the Scriptures themselves. Do not be fooled, talking about the Word is not the same as studying, teaching, or discussing the Word. A wise policy that will serve you well is this: "Always keep your finger in the text."

TEACHING LESS THAN THE WHOLE COUNSEL OF GOD

All of us like affirmation. It feels good when a particular lesson or message generates positive feedback. As a matter of fact, the wise speaker listens for feedback from his audience as one means of determining his effectiveness. However, not all subjects generate affirmation. Faithfulness to the whole counsel of God means dealing with the uncomfortable matters as well as those which are encouraging.

Teaching less than the whole counsel of God also occurs in response to issues of the day. Social ills and special causes arise and cry out to be addressed from a biblical standpoint. Yet when our teaching ministry becomes dominated by these special causes, the whole counsel of Scripture is lost.

Beware of the subtle pull toward overemphasis on any particular kind of subject. This is a classic example of a good thing which causes a bad thing when taken to the extreme.

Keep a close eye on the pattern of your teaching. Seek to open God's Word with the kind of balance with which He equipped it.

TEACHING HUMAN WISDOM

Another pull on our teaching ministry is that ambiguous pressure to be "contemporary." "Contemporary" might be defined as an emphasis on current self-help issues. God's Word offers perfect advice, but the pull is to discuss insights from psychology and sociology separate from the Word. Many have felt pressure to become pulpit counselors massaging human needs from the perspective of human wisdom. Yet when we abandon the Word we abandon our authority.

God has a great deal to say about the needs and predicaments man faces. His eternally relevant Word is the perfect guide, the perfect source, for accomplishing true life-change. The challenge for leaders is to bring the truth of God's Word to bear on the real issues of life. However, we need to stand guard against the temptation to adopt the methods and messages of the world in order to meet needs. You have the ultimate tool for real ministry: God's perfect Word.

USING THE WORD AS A CLUB

Though it may sound strange, our zeal for changed lives can become our own worst enemy. We desperately want people to respond to the Lord in growing obedience. We long to see the work of the kingdom expand through the work of God's people. As a result, we try to take on the role of the Holy Spirit and begin using the Word as a club to "encourage" obedience. When we allow ourselves to push people into feeling guilty, we are using the Word as a weapon. When we begin peppering our messages with "you ought to" and "you have to," we are clubbing our people with the Word.

Whenever God's Word is used that way, the good news of grace gets lost in the shuffle. Legalism and a performance mind-set are not far behind. If Jesus was able to say, "My yoke is easy, and my burden is light," then our teaching should reflect the same spirit. God's Word is not a stick with which we might browbeat His people into obedience. It is the Word of life. It is our extensive record of the depth of God's love for us. The manner in which we teach the Word should reflect the good news of the Word.

Guard yourself closely in this area. God's Word is the Sword of the Spirit, not the sword of the pastor! If the Spirit chooses to use His Sword to do surgery, that is His prerogative. It is inappropriate for us to attempt a work that is not ours to do.

PREVENTATIVE HEALTH POLICIES

In the last few decades medical science has gone to great lengths to teach us that physical health is more than an absence of illness. Staying healthy does mean treating signs of illness or disease, but it also means nurturing the vitality and strength of your body in general. Communicating the Word in a healthy manner is similar. We must watch for error and unhealthy trends. Yet at the same time there are a number of crucial health-building principles that ought to guide the way we open the Word. Here are three that will serve you well. Each can be summarized by a single word.

RELEVANCY

Every Sunday morning, every midweek service, and every Bible study is attended by people asking, "Does God have something to say to me today?" Some are asking this question consciously. Others have not formulated the words, but down inside the questions smolder: "Do God and His Word have something to say to me that will be relevant for my life? Does He understand the things that I face? And does He have insight for me today that will honestly make a difference?"

Relevance is one of the most important aspects of communicating the Word. Learning Greek and Hebrew will help a person study the Bible in its original languages. Studying commentaries will shed light on meaning, but once we have come to grips with meaning, we cannot afford to be satisfied. The next step of preparation is to ask ourselves, "How do the issues, principles, or examples of this passage relate to my audience?"

Being relevant does not mean that you adopt a song-and-dance routine in an attempt to be "contemporary." It means helping people discover ways that God and His Word connect with where they live. Every person in your ministry feels the need to discover how God through His Word relates to his daily life. When the Word is taught but not related to life, people return home empty. They had hoped God would speak to them, but now those unmet desires rattle around like echoes across an empty valley. Their expectations will become guarded. On the other hand, once you have adequately addressed the question of relevancy, people are primed for the next step—application.

APPLICATION

Whereas relevancy answers the question, "So what?" application answers the question, "Now what?" The principle is this: Every time the Word is opened people should understand what God is asking them to know, feel, or do. Without this final step in the teaching process, the message of the Word becomes short-circuited. Application is the means by which the Word becomes personalized in our lives. Or to say it a different way, it is not when I hear about the Word that I am changed but when I put it into practice in my life.

Application is perhaps the easiest aspect of communicating the Word to understand. There is nothing complex about it. Simply ask yourself the question, "Now what?" What should be done in response to the message of the Word you are teaching? What difference should it make in people's lives? Are there any actions that they should consider? Is there a clearer way of thinking that should be incorporated into their lives? Have any of their feelings been challenged or encouraged? Asking questions such as these will give you a handle on appropriate application.

One warning. The step of application may be simple to understand, but it is easy to omit. Time pressure during preparation can squeeze out the "think time" needed to determine helpful application. Sometimes those who teach become so caught up in the discoveries made during preparation that application seems too mundane. On another level, this portion of a message or Bible study may likely be a prime target for spiritual attack. If the evil one cannot prevent discussion about the Word, he will certainly work to prevent its application.

Make no mistake. Helping people apply the Word to their lives is not an optional activity. God's Word was meant to be studied and lived. God made that point long ago with these memorable words to Joshua: "This book of the law shall not depart from your mouth, but you shall meditate on it day and night, so that you may be careful to do according to all that is written in it" (Josh. 1:8, NASB).

MODELING

A third principle that promotes long-term health regarding the Word in your ministry is the principle of modeling. Simply stated, model an approach to the Word that people can learn from.

Over time, modeling Bible study methods that people can duplicate will have a profound effect. Those who sit under your ministry will learn to feed themselves. They will gain confidence knowing that they can discover truth from the Word themselves. They will seek to do what they have observed.

On the other hand, if our example communicates the need for special training and special tools, then our people will think they can't understand the Bible on their own. Unknowingly we might be encouraging a "Protestant dark ages" in our ministries.

STAYING FRESH AND PERSONAL

Over the long haul, everyone who serves in a teaching position—who knows the demand of constant preparation—knows the pressure of trying to stay fresh. It is a unique stress. No one is interested in opening the Scriptures and boring people. Standing before other people and putting them to sleep is the stuff of which nightmares are made. Within the heart of every teacher and leader is a deep desire to be fresh and personal.

Common sense dictates that the primary antidote to this pressure is to maintain your own healthy walk with the Lord. That is absolutely true. However, it is not the full extent of advice available. Here are two additional means by which you can actively seek to keep a fresh, personal perspective in your teaching.

LET GOD WORK IN YOUR LIFE

It sounds too simplistic, doesn't it? Let God work in your life. God's intent is that every aspect of life be pressed through the filter of His Word. You are seeking to help your people do just that in your teaching ministry. You should expect God to take you through various learning experiences so that you might be better equipped to teach people. The bottom line: God is committed to make His Word live in you so that through you it will live in others.

One man who speaks at conferences across the country told how this principle worked in his own life. He had been giving a particular series of messages that had a powerful impact and were being greatly used by God. One evening another man came up and said, "These messages have really been great. I just wish I could speak as well as you do." The speaker could only say to himself, *If you only knew the price I had to pay to learn those lessons, you might not be so eager.*

God is more committed to the impact of His Word than any of us are. As a result, He goes to great lengths to teach us firsthand how His principles work. He wants to teach us so that we might teach others with the certainty that comes from experience. Open yourself up to the work God wants to do in your life. Keep your heart tender. Even in the most trying situations, learn from His personal tutoring. Ask the Spirit of God to bring the Word to life in your experience so that you might speak with the confidence of one who knows it to be true. That which is experienced firsthand is always fresh and penetratingly personal.

READ

"Read any good books lately?" Sometimes this question provokes guilt. At other times it invites lively conversation about recent journeys through the printed page. But there is more to the matter of reading than healthy conversation. If we who attempt to feed others on a regular basis are to stay fresh, we have to be fed as well. Maintaining freshness over the long haul is difficult apart from continual input. Conferences and seminars can be helpful, but usually they are too few and far apart. Reading, on the other hand, provides a continual source of nourishment.

Regular reading also breaks the boundaries of our own limited experience. Every person has encountered a limited number and kind of experiences in life. Yet ministry requires bringing the light of the Word to bear on needs and experiences of all kinds, including those outside of our own understanding. What we read expands our ability to open the Word and make it relevant to all kinds of people.

The fact that you are reading this book says that you understand the value of reading. Yet how deeply ingrained is your habit? Look at your own life and schedule—have you cultivated the habit of regular reading? Time will always seem too short. Other things will always cry out for immediate attention, but break the deadlock. Carve out time to nourish your life and your ministry through reading. The freshness of your ministry and your ability to communicate the Word will see substantial benefits.[1]

Communicating the Word is so fundamental to ministry that none of us will ever outlive our need to increase our effectiveness. Look at the patterns you have developed. Have you been pulled off course by any of the lures of our age? Consciously begin to incorporate those principles that will increase impact publicly and personally.

PERSONAL ASSESSMENT

Having examined the six priorities for a healthy foundation for growth, it is time to personally examine their place in your ministry. All six are essential ingredients in a nurturing environment, so take time now to do some assessment.

Be honest. There is no one to impress and nothing to hide. Pray through the questions in this tool, and watch what the Lord shows you. Perhaps you might want to do this exercise together with some of the other leaders of your ministry. Admittedly, this is a subjective tool. However, it should help you pinpoint areas of strength and areas that need attention.

Evaluating Your Environment for Growth

ATMOSPHERE OF LOVE

1. On a scale of 1 to 100 (100 being the best), how would you rate your ministry as a place where people are loved?

2. On the same scale, how do you think a typical person in your ministry would rate the degree to which he or she feels loved?

3. On the same scale, how much do you truly love the people to whom you minister?

RELATIONAL MINISTRY

1. How many times during the week do you seek to make contact with people merely for the purpose of building a better relationship with them?

2. In what form is your contact usually made (phone, in person, and so on)?

3. List the names of people who regularly reach out to and get to know others.

CLEARLY COMMUNICATING CHRIST

1. Think back over the teaching in your ministry during the last six months. What percentage of the time has that teaching been devoted to helping people understand Christ more clearly?

2. What misconceptions of Christ are most prevalent in your congregation?

3. On what aspects of the person and work of Christ are your people most clear?

HEALTHY GROUP IMAGE

1. How strongly does the average person in your congregation believe God will work in your ministry? Use the scale below to mark your answer.

He has given up on us.	He might do a few things here.	He is ready to blow the doors off!

1------2------3------4------5------6------7------8------9------10

2. On a scale of 1 to 100 how proud do you think your people are to be a part of the ministry?

3. How often do you talk about your vision for what you believe God would like to do?

PRAYER BASE

1. What is being done to develop and maintain prayer support for the ministry and people of your body?

2. How much time do you spend in prayer for your ministry?

3. Who are the prayer warriors of your church?

TEACH THE WORD

1. Would you say that the teaching/preaching in your ministry teaches about the Word or teaches the Word itself? What evidence can you give to support your answer?

2. What percentage of the messages in your church include application portions so that people have ideas of how to apply what they learn?

3. What books have you read or what seminars have you attended recently to help you sharpen your teaching and preaching skills?

4. What aspect of the Word do people in your ministry most need to get a handle on?

Note

1. For further study see Larry Richards, *Creative Bible Teaching* (Chicago: Moody, 1970); Haddon Robinson, *Biblical Preaching: The Development and Delivery of Expository Messages* (Grand Rapids: Baker, 1980).

PHASE 2

EQUIPPING THE TEAM

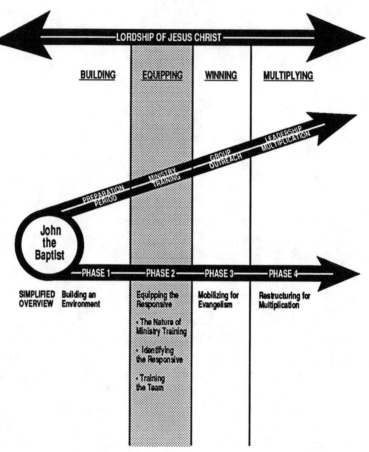

LORDSHIP OF JESUS CHRIST

| BUILDING | EQUIPPING | WINNING | MULTIPLYING |

PREPARATION PERIOD — MINISTRY TRAINING — GROUP OUTREACH — LEADERSHIP MULTIPLICATION

John the Baptist

PHASE 1 — PHASE 2 — PHASE 3 — PHASE 4

| SIMPLIFIED OVERVIEW | Building an Environment | Equipping the Responsive | Mobilizing for Evangelism | Restructuring for Multiplication |

• The Nature of Ministry Training

• Identifying the Responsive

• Training the Team

11

THE NATURE OF
MINISTRY TRAINING

Carl Wilson writes, "The step of Ministry Training [equipping] is critical to the expansion of any movement. At this point most organizations and local churches reach their peak. If they do not train believers other than the pastor to evangelize and build disciples, their expansion stops. The maximum potential is reached without a continuing growth and broadening impact. True multiplication occurs only when disciples are trained in evangelism and disciple-building. No matter how dynamic the leader, no matter how financially stable and well organized the church, expansion will not continue if people are not trained to minister."[1]

The ministry of Christ followed a plan that was radically simple and at the same time simply radical. His efforts followed a carefully crafted strategy to launch a ministry that would reach every corner of the globe. He began by building a foundation to initiate and sustain spiritual growth. As His followers grew spiritually He trained them to join Him in the work of His ministry. It seems too obvious doesn't it? Jesus' method demonstrates that after building a healthy foundation and putting in place the pieces that nurture growth, a leader begins to help people become equipped and involved in the work of ministry themselves.

At approximately the midpoint of His public ministry, Jesus called a few men for special training. His plan was to equip a team of followers to share in His work. Previously, His call had been, "Follow Me," but now He was saying, "Follow me, . . . and I will make you fishers of men" (Matt. 4:19). He would train them to minister. Jesus' work to equip a ministry team was no mere afterthought but a fundamental aspect of His strategy. Success in multiplying the breadth and depth of His ministry was dependent upon increasing the number of people able to do the work. [2]

We need to ask a few pointed questions. Does the pattern of Jesus' ministry look different from our own? How many churches chronically bemoan their need for more workers while doing little to equip them? Are our church calendars so over-programmed that no time or energy remains to equip people? Even in apparently healthy churches, how many people are able and actively working to reach their peers for Christ? This equipping phase is indispensable if we are to have Great Commission ministries.

Ministry training is about multiplication. It is also about obedience. In fact, it is impossible to grow in our ability to fulfill the Great Commission without equipping others to minister. Jesus showed us that healthy ministry is not merely an endless stream of activities generically designed to help Christians grow. He knew it was essential to get His disciples out on the front lines. And in the second phase of His ministry He began to do just that. Following His example and fulfilling His command means we must do the same.

At the core, ministry training is simply the process of equipping people to participate in the ministry of Christ. It is a matter of enabling believers to become reproducing disciples who live out the Great Commission. It means equipping believers to penetrate their sphere of influence in their own generation. The results of such a ministry can be seen in the lives of individuals, the scope of local ministry, and the impact on any given generation in any given community.

MINISTRY TRAINING AND INDIVIDUAL SPIRITUAL MATURITY

Lest this phase be misconstrued as merely a results-oriented endeavor, understand that the spiritual health and maturity of any believer is directly at stake. Earlier we defined discipling as an ongoing process in the life of every believer. It means meeting a person at his level of spiritual interest and helping him pursue Christ more completely and consistently. Ministry training provides the next challenge for the growing Christian.

Jesus' work to prepare and involve His followers in ministry was not just for the sake of the ministry at large but for their benefit as well. When He saw those who were responsive—those who had been growing in their faith and now were ready for more—He challenged them to become fishers of men. He knew that in order to continue growing in maturity they would need to begin giving their faith away. They needed to start using what they had learned.

How many Christians have you met who seem to have no joy in their spiritual lives? Do you know some who seem to have plateaued and become self-centered in their faith? Have you noticed new believers who take off like a rocket, then fizzle and settle into a nondynamic, nondemanding daily walk? Sadly, that seems to be the norm rather than the exception. The greatest news in the world is not even a big deal anymore. But the solution to spiritual complacency can be found in ministry training and involvement.

In Philemon 6 Paul lays it out. "I pray that you may be active in sharing your faith, so that you will have a full understanding of every good thing we have in Christ" (v. 6). Paul seems to say—and experience confirms—that if people don't get involved in sharing their faith, growth in Christ is hampered and spiritual stagnation begins. When people remain at the receiving level over a long period, they become critics, not servants. By contrast, in giving away your faith, you find it again.

Helping people grow as followers of Christ requires helping them begin to take steps into ministry. The tangible results
are their joy in faith, hunger for the Word, understanding of
Christ, and more. A discipling ministry helps growing believers
take this next step in their growth.

MINISTRY TRAINING AND THE GREAT COMMISSION

Whereas equipping and involving people in ministry has
profound effects on the individual believer, its impact and importance are as broad as the Great Commission itself.

When Jesus commanded us to make disciples of all nations, He was not only identifying a long-range goal; He was
clarifying the primary agenda for the church in every generation. Every church and group of believers in every generation
has been called to carry out the work of the Great Commission
in their own day and in their own community. In order to reach
any given generation for Christ, the believers within that generation must learn to reach their peers for Christ.

Ultimately, the goal of ministry training is to equip believers to reach their peers for Christ and help them grow in Him.
If people can be equipped to reach their peers, then they will be
able to reach their generation. Whether you work with high
school students, senior citizens, or any group in between, the
potential is incredible. People who have learned to reach their
peers will spend the rest of their lives growing in that ability.
On the other hand, if we fail to reach our peers, we fail to reach
our entire generation.

Yet we need to be honest. Working with one's own peers
—especially those with whom there is an ongoing relationship
—is the hardest ministry of all. The fears of rejection, failure,
or lack of credibility are intense. Short-term or non-peer ministry is generally less intimidating. But unless we equip our people to be fishers of men among their own generation, who else
will do it?

LEVELS OF MINISTRY

Although ministry training cannot happen apart from evangelism, ministry training is not merely a pseudonym for evangelism training. Equipping people to participate in every facet of making disciples is the issue. We in the contemporary church have accepted the idea that everyone need not participate in reaching out to their peers. We have allowed ourselves to believe that others will do it. That simply is not a biblical picture of the maturing disciple.

The full scope of this equipping process is perhaps best understood by identifying different levels of ministry involvement. By separating these levels, we are not implying that some things are important and others are not. Rather, these levels point out the increased "risk" involved. They also demonstrate the path of growth in personal ability. For practical purposes each level has been given a label.

M1: MINISTRY PROJECTS

The least threatening kind of ministry is the ministry project. It is generally an effort designed to serve nonpeers in a tangible manner. It includes such activities as delivering food, gathering clothing, building projects, or doing mechanical fix-it projects. Non-Christians can also do service projects, so the key to these activities becomes their twofold focus: (1) the people with the needs, and (2) the training of the workers. For many Christians this is an ideal way to begin reaching out to others.

M2: MINISTRY TO NONPEERS

This level is ministry to others within your culture but not your peer group (i.e., adults working with children, children or youth ministering to older adults, special ministries that travel to other churches). This is usually safe ministry. There is little risk of "getting stoned" and tremendous value and potential in this level of service.

M3: CROSS-CULTURAL MINISTRY TO NONPEERS

This level includes sharing the gospel and so becomes a bit more threatening. The key is that M3 ministry identifies efforts geared to another culture—often in another location. Included here would be short-term missions trips and work with "ethnic ministries" within your own metro area. Ministry at this level is still focused on those outside your normal sphere of influence. There is some safety in the fact that when the project is over, you can return home.

All three levels of ministry to this point focus primarily upon nonpeers. This is not to say that these are unimportant. However, there is a substantial increase in personal risk when reaching out to one's peers. Growth as a disciple necessitates the ability to reproduce ourselves among our peers. The next four levels move us into this kind of ministry.

M4: MINISTRY TO BELIEVING PEERS: EDIFICATION

Caring for and serving believers within the body. This level of ministry may include formal or informal positions of influence such as teaching a class, leading a Bible study, lay counseling ministry, and so on.

M5: MINISTRY TO NONBELIEVING PEERS: EXPANSION

At this level there is intentional effort to build better relationships with non-Christian friends. Just as Jesus was known to be a "friend of sinners," so the person at this level is seeking to befriend the unchurched. Although most of us know how to be a friend, few Christians have significant relationships with the unchurched. This level of ministry training helps believers become a "friend to sinners" and to do so with a redemptive purpose.

M6: MINISTRY TO NONBELIEVING PEERS: EXTENSION

Here evangelism and discipleship occur on a peer level. A person at this point is able to bring the gospel into his or her relationships with the unchurched. In fact, because the gospel is carried through the vehicle of a relationship there is also a natural vehicle for "postnatal care." As we said, ministry training is not merely a pseudonym for evangelism training. The point is that people learn to bring the gospel to their peers and then help them begin growing in their faith.

M7: MINISTRY TO NONBELIEVING PEERS: EXPLOSION

We label this level "explosion" because this is the stage at which people develop personal strategies for reaching and discipling others. Those at the M5 and M6 levels take advantage of existing relationships with the unchurched. But the person at M7 is actively working to increase his impact in his sphere of influence. He is seeking to initiate relationships through any number of natural vehicles in life—work, school, children's sports, and so on. Ministry can become exciting as students begin reaching out to other students or as Little League parents start reaching parents of other team members. Pilots can begin reaching pilots. Teachers, police officers, executives all reach out into their sphere of influence. The possibilities are endless.

Perhaps the most important thought underlying this discussion is this: God is anxious to use every follower of Christ to reach his or her world. Growth as a disciple of Christ—by design—includes growing into involvement in ministry. When Jesus took His disciples aside and commanded them to make disciples of all nations, He made that point eternally clear. Reach out to the men and women of your world, and walk them down this path we have shown you. Help them grow as disciples—"followers of Me"—who are able to reach others.

For some reason the church today has grown satisfied involving people in the first few levels of ministry, as if there
were nothing more to be done. As a result, cross-cultural ministry (the M3 level) is seen as the pinnacle of ministry. Perhaps
this is why the average church in America sees less than a 3
percent conversion growth rate a year. Meanwhile our effectiveness in reaching our own communities in our own generation has been minimal. The issue is not that these other ministries are less significant. Rather, God's plan for every believer
is to learn to reproduce themselves in their own sphere of influence, even if their primary position of ministry is within the
body.

Surely, there are still unanswered questions: How do you
know who should be equipped for ministry? What should be
done to train people for ministry? What about the many people
who are uncomfortable with the claim that this is God's plan for
everyone? Doesn't this diminish the significance of ministry
that takes place within the body? What does this emphasis on
reaching your peers say about missions?

Let's tackle the last two questions now, and we will address the others in the next few chapters. Missionaries have
been uniquely called by God to bring the gospel to another people group. Doing that effectively means building relationships
with people so that, in effect, they become the missionary's
peers. It also means that his or her approach to ministry is designed to help new national believers reach their own peers and
build a full-orbed ministry within their own culture.

In a different vein, what would we say to the woman who
feels called by God to serve others through the nursery? Have
her twenty-three years of service been for naught? Not in the
least! It is appropriate to invest priority effort in a ministry that
fits the way God has made you. However, even though a person's primary ministry position is, for example, in the nursery,
that does not exclude him from learning to reach his peers. In
fact, efforts to reach the unchurched can inject a whole new
impetus to ministry among believers.

Imagine how a heart for the lost and ability to bring the gospel to others might benefit the ministry of our friend in the nursery. She has an incredible opportunity to touch the lives of young families. Frequently she is the primary contact for the unchurched who attend a service. The more someone grows in his ability to win and build others for Christ, the greater his contribution to ministry.

Ministry training is a never-ending process. Equipping people for ministry is part of helping them grow in faith and obedience to Christ. It is also the means by which we mobilize the Body to fulfill the Great Commission. Clearly, the disciple-making process includes reaching the lost. It also includes building up believers in their faith and equipping them to participate actively and aggressively in the process of building others.

Notes

1. Carl Wilson, *With Christ in the School Building* (Grand Rapids: Zondervan, 1976), p. 101.

2. Jesus moved to the region of Capernaum as a ministry headquarters about this time.

12

IDENTIFYING THE RESPONSIVE

Discussing the process of equipping people for ministry is easy as long as we stick to generalities. However, coming to grips with reality means answering pragmatic questions. Who should be equipped? How will we recognize them? And when we find them, what do we do to equip them? For now, let's address how we will recognize the people we want to equip.

As always, our example is Christ. His early ministry consisted primarily of relationships with a few in the Judean countryside. During this time He was making contact with a variety of people. Reaching out wherever He went, He was calling all to repentance and faith (Mark 1:14-15). He was also watching for and nurturing those who were responsive to Him. Although we typically think of Jesus' ministry as being done in the company with the twelve, they were not appointed at the beginning.

When Jesus called these men to follow Him and become "fishers of men," He was bringing them together for special equipping. He moved into the Galilee region and entered a ministry training phase with them. The time was right for them to grow not only in their commitment to Him but in their ability to serve Him.

The strategy of Christ should be our own strategy. That is, we should be watching for people who are ready for more. We should be looking for those who are responsive—responsive to Christ and to our ministries. They will be the people who no longer want only to be ministered to but who want to minister to others. They will not be content to be served because they want to serve others. Instead of being satisfied by being taught, they are hungry to teach others. In short, they are becoming others-oriented.

To state it another way, we should look for people who want more—who have been growing in Christ. Having been involved in activities that help them grow, they now have a gnawing desire to contribute. There is a sense of fullness in their lives that is overflowing.

Profile of the Responsive

How will you recognize those who are ready for more? Do not be dismayed; this is not as difficult to figure out as it may sound. There is no denying that it is a subjective process, but under the guidance of the Holy Spirit it is neither haphazard nor unclear.

The following four criteria will help you identify those who are responsive. Granted, the criteria are not scientifically measured; they are measured cumulatively. When you look at a person whose life reflects significant aspects of all four traits, you are looking at a prime candidate. (These criteria are not new but are so worthwhile they deserve our renewed attention.)

FAITHFUL

Faithfulness to the Lord is demonstrated through our willingness to strive for consistency as we follow Him. None of us is absolutely consistent, nor are we 100 percent faithful. But faithfulness can be seen in a person's desire to live in a manner that will please the Lord. A person who is growing in Christ will naturally grow in his desire to please Him through his actions.

In addition to faithfulness to the Lord, look for faithfulness to the Body of Christ. Is the person demonstrating faithfulness in his involvement in the programs of the body? Is he showing an increased faithfulness toward people within the body? Is he tangibly expressing willingness to be responsible for certain tasks? These expressions of faithfulness demonstrate a person's responsiveness to Christ Himself, as well as to the ministry of Christ expressed through the church.

As your ministry develops, you will want to move people into positions of leadership. It is only appropriate that those to whom you entrust responsibilities are ones who have a track record of demonstrated faithfulness. Therefore, encouraging faithfulness as part of the equipping process will pave the way for future leadership.

AVAILABLE

After faithfulness comes availability. We see availability in Isaiah when he cries, "Here am I. Send me!" (Isa. 6:8). It is an attitude of openness to the control and direction of God's Spirit. The person who is available desires God to use him however and whenever He would like to. If God's agenda means a slight change of plans, so be it. The person who is available to the Lord has combined a hunger to be used with a willingness to be flexible.

Availability should be demonstrated on a practical level. Someone may demonstrate a responsive heart and by every measure show readiness for ministry training and yet be unavailable because of his schedule. There are times in everyone's life when he is temporarily unavailable, and leaders need to recognize this. On the other hand, when you encounter unavailability because of schedules, it may be a good time for evaluation. If a person's schedule does not allow him to participate, then one of three things is probably true. First, now is not the time for him to be equipped for ministry. Second, his schedule is out of control, and it's time to do surgery on the commitment load. Or your plan for ministry training is too rigidly structured and needs to flex in order to better accommodate others.

TEACHABLE

The attitude of being teachable is one of the most important qualities a believer can ever cultivate. It is a hunger to learn. It is a willingness to be corrected that comes from admitting how much growth he needs. In contrast, a person who is unteachable stands unbendable in the false confidence that he has arrived. The person who is teachable recognizes that every one of us has so far to go to become like Christ that in many ways we are all just beginners. Like Paul, the believer will always say, "Not that I have already obtained all this . . . but I press on" (Phil. 3:12).

An appetite for the Word and a zeal to grow in godliness characterize the one who is teachable. These qualities make him a prime candidate for ministry training. Have you ever wondered why Jesus did not choose any of the Pharisees for ministry training? Possibly He saw in their lives a hard, unteachable spirit. His disciples on the other hand, although "uneducated men," were fully teachable. They were willing to try anything and give up everything in order to follow Christ. Those who will follow Christ and become fishers of men today must be men and women, like the disciples, who are teachable.

ENTHUSIASTIC

A healthy enthusiasm about the work of God is a sign of a growing relationship with Him. Enthusiasm is a willingness to speak about the work of God in one's life. The one who is enthused about God talks about the things he is learning from the Word, the answers to prayer he is experiencing, and the lessons he is learning from others of the Body. That is not to say that people need to be cheerleaders constantly waving pom poms to arouse the crowd. Different personalities demonstrate enthusiasm differently. In all cases you might say that godly enthusiasm is the result of a healthy, growing relationship with the Lord that keeps bursting out.

Look for enthusiasm about your local ministry as well. A person who is to be equipped for ministry within your local body should have a healthy enthusiasm for it. He should own the vision and be excited about its potential. That is not to say he has a blind allegiance to all you are doing or that he thinks everything is perfect. Nonetheless he has enthusiasm about the work God is doing through your church or ministry.

THE CONSTANT DILEMMA

All of this talk about identifying people for ministry training may make good sense, but it may also generate certain internal frustration. Most ministries feel a personnel squeeze. Programs are understaffed. Plans for the future are left on the drawing table for lack of manpower. "This all sounds fine and good," you might say, "but to start up a new effort now might drain away the best people we have!"

Could the reason for this chronic problem be that we have neglected the equipping phase of ministry? Granted, this is not a magic wand to be waved over your ministry to instantly solve all personnel needs. Nor is it a quick-fix salve to be massaged into troubled ministries. Jesus' pattern demonstrates careful building for the long haul. By working to equip people to serve, we will begin meeting our need for additional personnel as well as the needs of individuals who are ready for more.

Rather than look at ministry training as an additional program to add on, why not make it a natural part of existing ministries? Instead of assuming that people have to be pulled *out* of their areas of involvement, ministry training is best done "on the job." Within every sphere of ministry, leaders could be watching for those who are growing in Christ and are ready for more. Then within the ongoing relationships of that ministry area they could begin equipping a team. Existing ministries could make ministry training a specific goal for those who are already serving. Rather than allow people to merely maintain existing programs, their involvement could become a training vehicle. After all, ministry training is not accomplished in a classroom. It is essential to walk a person through the levels of ministry as outlined in chapter 11.

At the same time, the solution to our personnel needs is really spiritual. The Master identified those into whom He would pour out His life—those to whom He would hand over His ministry—by prayer. In a generation accustomed to marketing gimmicks and well-rehearsed sales pitches, prayer lacks tangible appeal. Yet the fact is that prayer is perhaps the most tangible tool in our arsenal.

Jesus' example is penetrating. When it was time for Him to formally identify twelve disciples for special training, He spent the entire night in prayer (Luke 6:12-13). There was Jesus, the one with perfect wisdom, the one who knew the hearts of men, and He needed to pray about it. Later He pointed out the magnitude of the harvest into which He had called His disciples. Then He gave them this instruction: "Ask the Lord of the harvest, therefore, to send out workers into his harvest field" (Matt. 9:38). By example and instruction He calls us to depend on prayer as our primary means for finding the people we need.

EAGER PATIENCE

Are there men and women in your ministry who have demonstrated responsiveness? Based on these criteria, are there people who are ready to enter a new phase of growth as disciples of Christ? The need before every leader in the Body of Christ is to open his eyes and begin eagerly looking for responsive people. Meeting people wherever they are spiritually means watching for those who need to learn to minister. It means helping those who have been receivers learn to give to others. This process will not only help people grow as disciples, but it will begin to open the doors for greater expansion and penetration by our ministries.

A word of caution. Just as it is possible to overlook the need to identify the responsive, it is also possible to move too quickly. Whereas the wise leader is always on the lookout for those who are ready for more, he is also patient to wait for the Lord to raise them up in due time. Guard yourself so that impatience does not lead to premature action.

Jesus' example is incredible. He knew His ministry would only last for three years, yet He waited until approximately the halfway point before beginning ministry training. If He could wait, we can too. Open your eyes, and start looking for those whom God is nurturing for potential ministry training. Examine their lives for evidence of faithfulness, availability, teachability, and enthusiasm. When you see these qualities and you sense a green light from the Spirit of God, it will be time to begin specifically equipping them for ministry.

13

TRAINING THE TEAM

The goal of any Biblical model of life-change must be to accomplish a fundamental shift in how a person uses his or her energies.

—Kevin Huggins

Ministry training is the process of helping people shift the use of their energies. This chapter will attempt to clarify how to go about the equipping process. You should be encouraged by the relative simplicity of this process. Yet you will probably be a little overwhelmed by the fact that the task of ministry training is endless.

One of the common mistakes of the equipping process is that it lacks an intentional approach. Though leaders have a great desire for people to be trained for ministry, they have no specific means to make it happen. There is a universal desire to "mature" believers in Christ but a perennial lack of systems to facilitate that growth. One could assume we believe that once started on their way, people will learn all they need to know as they go. However, the pattern of Christ demonstrates the need for special effort and attention. That is the first major ingredient of an effective equipping ministry.

The ministry training process can be divided into four primary categories, which should serve as constant reference points. All need to be in place simultaneously; they are not consecutive steps. The guidelines of ministry training are: *impart your life, challenge people to involvement, support your team with training,* and *keep your focus clear.*

IMPART YOUR LIFE

The greatest stumbling point in training others for ministry is *fear* of not knowing what to do. Repeatedly people ask, "What should we teach?" "What do I do?" "Where do I start?" Answering practical questions is the next step in our journey. But there is no magic curriculum. The training should be as interpersonal as any other aspect of ministry.

Here is a scenario. For weeks you prayed for discernment, anxious to identify those who needed to be challenged for ministry training. You told everyone about your plans so that no one would feel alienated. Even someone you had never thought would be interested in ministry training expressed a desire to be included. It all seemed to go so smoothly and simply. Until today.

Today is the first meeting with the new "team members," and now an unsettling fear has blown in. What exactly should you do with these eager people? What should you teach them? How should your time be spent? On the one hand so many important matters need to be covered that choosing a place to start is impossible. On the other hand, you are struck by the feeling that you don't know enough to lead such an endeavor. If you're lucky, no one will show up, and then you'll be off the hook—for the moment.

Nowhere does it say that ministry training must be a formally structured classroom experience. As a matter of fact, the classroom is probably where the least amount of time should be spent. However, an illustration such as the one above pinpoints the level of inadequacy or frustration many feel here. Learning to effectively minister to others is a lifelong journey. But assisting others in that journey is not impossible.

The primary teaching focus of ministry training is simply this: *impart your life*. In fact, you could say that the very essence of discipling is imparting your life to others. Paul described this process when he summarized his ministry to the Thessalonians: "We loved you so much that we were delighted to share with you not only the gospel of God but our lives as well" (1 Thess. 2:8).

Jesus went so far as to say that whenever you are engaged in teaching and equipping another person you are engaged in imparting your life to him. You don't even have a choice! "A student is not above his teacher, but everyone who is fully trained will be like his teacher" (Luke 6:40). The process of training others for ministry means helping them learn to imitate Christ even as you are learning to do the same.

"Fine and good, but that still doesn't tell me what to say to those I am trying to train for ministry!" The answer to that question lies in what God has taught you. Rather than trying to teach your ministry team what "the experts" might have to say—forcing you to "fake it" and teach what you haven't personally mastered—teach what God has taught you. Use those things that God has built into your Christian life and experience as your curriculum.

An amazing thing happens when you do this. You will find that frequently the things God has taught you are exactly the things He wants to use in the lives of others. This approach forces us to acknowledge that we are not adequate to train people alone. We need the help of other Christians. However, this is exactly the central truth of New Testament discipleship—the Body of Christ rubbing off on each other!

To help you get started, here is a simple exercise. Take a blank piece of paper and a pencil, and list everything God has taught you to bring you to where you are today. This list can cover everything from personal insights gleaned from the Word to effective ministry and leadership skills. You have had to learn how to study the Word, organize your priorities, overcome fear, walk by faith, organize programs, and so forth. Write it all down. When you are done write across the top, "A Place to Start." Prioritize five of the most important on your list. That is a valuable place to start as you train others for ministry.

CHALLENGE PEOPLE TO INVOLVEMENT

In this information age we are prone to look for answers in the form of more facts. That tendency infiltrates the church as well. We view the training process as another opportunity to communicate more information. We think that if a person is bombarded with enough data, he or she will be adequately equipped. However, it does not work that way.

Do you remember learning to drive a car with manual transmission? There you were, ready to get behind the wheel. You'd watched others do it for years, and it always looked so simple. And now your father was trying to tell you what to do. You probably weren't really listening. After all, you already knew everything.

Finally, you pull away from the curb. Watch the road. Check your mirrors. Monitor your speed. Anticipate other drivers. Check your blind spot. Stay away from that slow car on the right. It's more complex than you anticipated. How is that gas gauge? Whew! You take a deep breath and settle down. Oh no, time to shift again. Grind, chug, jerk . . . the clutch will never be the same again. After a few tense moments of actual experience you have become a much more interested learner.

Ministry training needs to focus on involvement for the same reason. Once a person is *involved* in ministry he is more eager to learn. He also gains a filter through which to better understand instruction. Therefore those who train others for ministry must challenge them to take the risk of involvement. This challenge ought to be appropriate for their maturity level. In fact, part of the rationale behind identifying seven different levels of ministry is to assist leaders in guiding and challenging people appropriately.

As you challenge people to participate in ministry, two things are essential to make the most of their experience. The first is to know where you are headed. Ultimately the goal of ministry training is to equip people to become effective in doing the work of the Great Commission among their peers. As people are challenged to take greater risks, they need to know there is purpose to the risk. Ministry to another cultural group at home or somewhere else can provide training in evangelism and exposure to the power of the gospel. Involvement in ministry at any level is significant in its own right, but for the leader who knows where he is headed it becomes a vehicle for training.

A second key for maximizing the value of participation is to give people the freedom to fail. Failure is always hard, yet we usually learn more from our mistakes than we do from our successes. It is crucial that leaders give people the room to fail and then provide encouragement to help them learn from failures. Help them clarify what specific steps could be taken to change things for the better. Help them discover the truth of Paul's insight about how God uses us in our weakness. Moments of failure can be prime opportunities for personalized instruction and encouragement.

Support Your Team with Training

Although the preceding discussion may seem to deny the importance of intentional training, that is not the case. We are so prone to jump into an academic feed-em-more-data mind-set that we have to force the issue of actual involvement first.

Cursory examination of Jesus' ministry reveals that He took great care to make sure His disciples were equipped with a clear understanding of His ministry. At times He allowed events to speak for themselves. At other times He pulled the men aside to debrief them about what had taken place. Some of His teaching was directed specifically at them. Some of Jesus' comments to the Pharisees and to others were purposely given in hearing of His ministry team. And there were endless days on the road when He had the chance to share, review, and clarify an untold number of principles. Those who serve in ministry today have no less a need to be equipped with insights and skills to serve effectively.

Training people for ministry may or may not need to take on a formal structure. Following the example of Christ, there are clearly a wide variety of ways to train people. Often training can be done on an informal and individual basis. One-on-one situations sometimes work best. At other times it is helpful to bring groups of people together. Including a training time in the meetings held by already functioning ministry teams works well also.

One rule of thumb is to use only as much formal structure as necessary. For those who lead specific segments of ministry, the team to be equipped may be easy to identify. Those who are leaders over a broad ministry, such as a whole church, may find this process a bit more complex. Regardless of your situation, you will want to develop enough structure to carry out consistent training. You will want to identify, challenge, and then equip those who are ready to grow in ministry.

Helping people understand the principles of ministry and helping them increase the level of their ministry skills are both objectives of formal training. We need people who are both thinkers and doers. Benefits of this intentional effort will be not only in the area of ministry effectiveness; people will gain the confidence of being prepared and the encouragement of being supported.

KEEP YOUR FOCUS CLEAR

Over time it is common for ministries to lose sight of the equipping process and settle into "project mode." Project mode is that approach which sees a ministry effort as an end in itself. People are being used to complete tasks, staff service projects, or fill program slots, but they are not imparting their lives to others. The heart and opportunity for ministry training are replaced by something that just has to get done. Let's examine some differences between a project mentality and a true ministry mind-set.

Project Mentality	Ministry Mind-set
Invest life and energy to complete a task	Invest life and energy in a person to make a spiritual difference
Focus on time or resources needed	Focus on imparting of life
Spiritual preparation a low priority	Spiritual preparation a high priority
Program/task oriented	People oriented

In one other area it is essential to keep our focus clear. Ministry training must include evangelism. A person cannot be fully trained to do the work of the Great Commission within his or her sphere of influence without evangelism training. Yet there is often a breakdown at this point. In some cases the pressing demands of maintaining local ministry consume the time and energy needed to involve people creatively in evangelism. In other cases—probably the vast majority—there is such discomfort with traditional evangelistic methods that most people give up. Put simply, people don't like evangelism, and they don't believe God will use them.

Granted, everyone is not a gifted evangelist. However, participation in reaching the lost is God's intent for every believer. Could it be that our corporate methods for assisting, encouraging, and enabling evangelism are the culprit? If we were to develop new approaches that truly helped people reach their friends, could we change this pattern of resistance?

The third phase of Jesus' ministry occurred hand in hand with His effort to train His team. In the following chapters as we discuss the next phase of ministry we will explore principles

of outreach that can make a difference. In fact, you may find
that a new approach to evangelism opens many doors for the
people of your ministry. However you approach outreach, your
success in ministry training must include involvement in evangelism.

The questions before you at this point are twofold: Are
you eager to multiply the depth and breadth of your ministry?
And, are you eager to build a ministry that meets people at
their point of spiritual need and helps them continue to grow as
disciples? Both of these desires call for an effort to begin training people for ministry. It may seem demanding at present, but
it is also full of joy.

A word of encouragement. When it comes to ministry, the
most astounding thing is the fact that God is willing to allow any
of us to serve in any capacity at all. He has chosen to take the
weak and the flawed, the awkward and the bungled, and
through it all accomplish the eternal work of His kingdom. We
have the opportunity to multiply that work by walking with other people as they grow to discover the privilege and power of
ministry. The grace of God which allows us to serve Him
makes it exciting to invite others to participate too.

As you see a team become equipped and involved, be prepared to watch your ministry propelled further than you ever
dreamed.

PHASE 3

WINNING THE MASSES

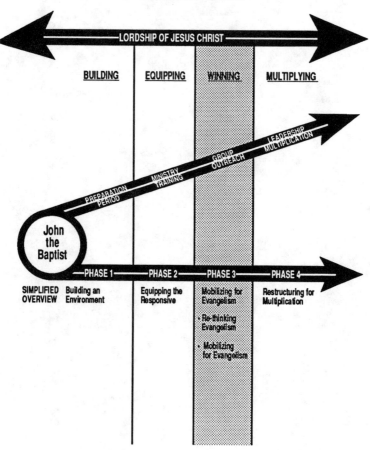

14

RETHINKING EVANGELISM

The majority of [Christians] believe they cannot be successful in sharing their faith.
                                        —The Barna Group

A certain ritual—an adventure really—takes place every fall in many parts of the country. If you have ever driven through Wisconsin, for example, during Thanksgiving week you know firsthand what this rite of fall is all about. Deer hunting season is open, and for a short period of time it seems that nothing else matters.

Thousands upon thousands of virile warriors forage through the woods for what they hope will be "my deer." Dressed warmly, doing double duty on the coffee intake, and proudly wearing the essential blaze-orange outer gear, these men and women pursue their goal with gusto. Many a hunter will return home with his prize strapped to the top of his car. Others return with spell-binding stories about what almost happened. All return home with glazed eyes and plans for better tactics next year.

Is our understanding of evangelism akin to "spiritual deer hunting season"? Even the title of this chapter seems to convey the idea of mobilizing for military maneuvers. The typical church's plan to get on the stick evangelistically involves the same kind of efforts as deer hunters.

For months they prepare themselves. They check and re-check their weapons. They arrange their schedules. They gather together with a few trusted friends for some form of pep talk. Finally, when the time is right, they thrust themselves into the target-rich environment, looking to make a kill. They search for someone with whom they can share the good news of Christ. When it is all over, they put their weapons away and return to the safety of normal life to share stories about "the one that got away."

There *is* a place for special training and witnessing programs. They have done great good for many people. However, somewhere along the way the bulk of the church has grown comfortable viewing itself as a safe haven—a fortress of security—in a hostile world. We have lost sight of our calling to be an intentionally aggressive redemptive agency. Efforts designed to reach the lost have become the special activities of a few hard-core types instead of the norm for all. Evangelistic activity has become a special endeavor, perhaps for a special season, but not standard operating procedure.

Although no one denies the importance of evangelism, the vast majority of believers are uncomfortable with the idea that all of us should be active in it. People get fired up about the prospects of outreach—so long as someone else carries the ball. Rethinking our approach and our perspective is essential. We need to develop a workable corporate strategy that will mobilize people for evangelism and assist them along the way.

The Goals of an Outreach Ministry

Every aspect of a disciple-making ministry is connected to and interdependent with evangelism. The following four goals of an outreach ministry will make that interdependence readily apparent. These goals will provide the clear purpose needed to drive your efforts to mobilize the body for evangelism.

1. TO REACH THE MASSES

The reigning theme of Scripture is that God is in the business of reconciling men and women to Himself. He is passionate about that pursuit; the Old Testament called Him "jealous." The New Testament reveals the same heartbeat in the ministry of Christ, who said the reason He came was to seek and save those who were lost.

A ministry committed to the Great Commission takes seriously the need and the command to take the gospel to all men. If we are in the business of helping people become disciples of Christ, we must first help them become followers of Him! Whether it is through intensive efforts of personal evangelism or through creative outreach-oriented corporate events, our mandate is to reach the masses who are lost without a Savior.

There is another side to this mandate for evangelism, which we frequently neglect. In the words of Christ, "The harvest is plentiful" (Matt. 9:37). How often have you heard the need for evangelism discussed in light of a promised plentiful harvest? On the contrary, we tend to present evangelism as if we don't expect many to respond. We are often more prepared to shake the dust off of our feet than to rejoice at the size of the harvest. But Jesus promised that the harvest is plentiful!

Churches such as Willow Creek Community Church outside of Chicago and Saddleback Valley Community Church in southern California are living proof of this promise. Both of these churches, as well as scores of others, have been built upon true conversion growth. They have taken God's promise of a plentiful harvest seriously and have developed systems to deliver the good news effectively. It is time for all of us to step out, anxious to see the words of Jesus fulfilled.

2. TO INTENTIONALLY HELP BELIEVERS REACH THEIR FRIENDS

Even though we are discussing the need to corporately facilitate evangelism, we are not discussing sterile, impersonal effort. Evangelism happens in the context of interpersonal relationships. It happens when one believer allows God to use him as salt and light within his own sphere of influence. All too frequently evangelistic programming takes people out of their spheres of influence. But personal friends and acquaintances from any arena of life form the most natural environment in which to begin reaching out. Our friends are our personal mission field.

However, it is naive to think that every Christian will be able to reach his or her friends without assistance. For this reason special outreach programs should be designed to help people reach their friends.

There is clearly room for nonpeer evangelism. But that is only a portion of our task. Rather than pulling people out of their natural relationships we should be helping them reach those with whom they are already close. In fact, we should work hard to make it easy to reach out to unchurched friends. The sky is the limit in terms of approaches that might be taken.

Our efforts to help people reach their friends will also help them grow in Christ. Aiding people as they reach out to others helps them live in obedience. It helps them grow in their ability to personally carry on the work of Christ.

3. TO FURTHER TRAIN THE TEAM

Jesus made a deliberate effort to develop people and to develop His ministry at an appropriate pace. Though His ministry was consistently characterized by personal evangelism, it was after He had His team in place that He moved into large-scale outreach (see Mark 1). Being concerned with maximum stability and penetration He waited until the groundwork had been laid and His team was ready to move. His move to Capernaum and into mass evangelism at this third stage was possible because His team was ready. And it was necessary in order to further train His team.

Cultivating a heart for the lost was something Jesus had sought to do among His disciples from the beginning. But His move into an aggressive outreach phase of ministry would provide them with the further hands-on training they needed. Training in ministry is not complete if people are only prepared to work with believers. Those who are being equipped for ministry need the growth and exposure that comes from involvement in evangelism. They also need to hone their ability to reach their peers if they are to become reproducing disciples.

4. TO GENERATE A MOVEMENT

The fourth goal motivating an outreach ministry is the desire to create a movement that genuinely penetrates the lost world around us. For some reason many contemporary churches have grown content with church growth apart from evangelism. Reginald Bibby, writing about the church in Canada, hits the nail on the head about the American church as well with these words:

> It is hard to say, but it needs to be said nonetheless. When evangelicals talk about their successes in evangelism they are frequently inaccurate at best and dishonest at worst. For too long, many evangelicals have equated church growth with outreach, failing to differentiate between their net numerical gains and their success in reaching nonprofessing Christians. . . . Seven out of every 10 new members come from other evangelical churches, while two in 10 are the children of evangelicals. Only about one in 10 new members come from outside of the evangelical community.[1]

A movement is like a snowball. It begins small, picking up size and speed as it rolls. As your ministry begins to mobilize for evangelism, those who lead the way initiate a real movement. A growing movement based on evangelism will foster greater enthusiasm, greater participation, greater expectation, and greater impact. The more who join in a "movement of the

Lord," the greater your ability to reach people. In many cases, it is at this point that a ministry explodes.

FRESH THINKING ABOUT EVANGELISM

Let's be honest. On one hand, discussing evangelism is akin to talking about Mom and apple pie. Every Christian cheers its importance and its potential. Yet at the same time, evangelism is to many people like ingesting medicine—about as much fun as having a tooth pulled. Sadly, somewhere along the line most Christians have been bludgeoned by the hammer of guilt over evangelism. Attempts to call believers to evangelism have left a repugnant taste in their mouths. Even if it's important, people would rather avoid it.

It is intolerable for us to remain content, allowing this inadequate view of evangelism to continue. Evangelism should be positive, *not* guilt-ridden. It should be joy-filled, not burdensome. If it is true that evangelism is the process of sharing the greatest news in the history of mankind, then it should be fun to do so! With a harvest that is plentiful and the Spirit of God who is anxious to use us, the problem we face is our delivery, the means we use in trying to communicate the message.

Conquering our lack of enthusiasm—often outright resistance—requires what could be called "an everyman approach to evangelism." That is, we need to create an approach that could work for every believer and has the potential to reach any nonbeliever. Here are four principles to prod your thoughts about an "everyman" approach.

EVANGELISM IS A TEAM SPORT

If you were to go to your local Christian bookstore and peruse all the books on evangelism, what would you find? In nearly every case they are discussing "personal evangelism." Corporate strategies are limited primarily to organized training programs that equip people to go out sharing their faith one-on-

one. But what about the fact that the Body of Christ has been designed to carry on the ministry of Christ collectively?

You see, typically our approach to personal evangelism puts the entire load of bringing someone to Christ into one person's lap. Additionally, our approach generally focuses on non-peers. There is certainly nothing wrong with these methods, and great good has come through them. However, most Christians and most ongoing relationships would benefit from a different approach. As the Body of Christ we ought to be functioning as a team. We should be providing opportunities and personal assistance to one another in our efforts to reach non-believing friends.

Here is how this principle worked in the life of one man—we'll call him Dave. Raised in a non-Christian home, Dave had a heart for evangelism. Eager to serve the Lord, Dave went to Bible college where his training included extensive work in evangelism. Later he earned his Master's degree in evangelism and even wrote materials to train others in sharing their faith. In spite of all his training, however, he could not lead his Oriental neighbors to Christ.

Over the course of several years Dave and his wife had prayed constantly for their neighbors. They had them over for dinner. They went out socially. And they talked about spiritual things. Yet for some reason the neighbor did not trust in the message that Dave had worked so hard to share.

Now in a different community in a new home, Dave and his wife realize what they should have done. They should have helped their neighbors meet and get to know other Christians. Typically an unbeliever needs to have more than five meaningful contacts with a number of Christians before he or she will begin to trust the message of the gospel.

In their new home Dave has begun to rely more on the Body of Christ to help reach his neighbors. One neighbor needed some landscaping done, so Dave quickly connected him with a Christian landscaper from his church. Another time his neighbor needed some carpentry work done, so Dave introduced him to a carpenter he knew—who just happened to attend his church, too. You know, Dave's neighbor has hit it off better with these other Christians than with Dave. Yet together they are each sharing and caring for this man. They are also beginning to see him open up to spiritual things.

None of this is to say that Dave's first neighbor would have responded to the gospel had other believers been involved. But the odds are that the opportunities would have been greater had they taken a team approach.

This is just a glimpse—just a scratch on the surface—of all that can be done when the whole body works together as a team. Creative events, activities centered around shared interests, special services, and many other options could all be used to help individual believers reach their friends.

EVANGELISM IS A PROCESS, NOT AN EVENT

Somehow people have come to believe that evangelism is a highly packaged, highly structured event. It means sharing the words of the gospel, giving an invitation, and asking for a decision, right? Actually the redemptive process is almost always broader than that. Usually when a person responds to the invitation of the gospel, it is because seeds had been planted long before. Those seeds have been carefully cultivated by different people and events under the guiding hand of the Holy Spirit. The point of response is definitely the exciting point of new birth, but it is only one point in the redemptive process.[2]

TARGET PEOPLE IN ALL PHASES OF THE DECISION PROCESS

Since evangelism is a process not an event, methods and programs should target people in all phases of the decision process. Efforts designed to reach the unbeliever who is not yet curious or hungry for spiritual things need to focus on cultivating the soil. Once the hardened soil has been tilled you can continue to build bridges into his life by planning ways to sow the seeds. At some point as this unbelieving person is exposed to Christ, there will hopefully come a time to harvest the fruit. Until a person is ready to make a decision for Christ, you continue cultivating and sowing. Outreach programming that only targets the point of harvest is bypassing everyone at other stages of the redemptive process.

FRIENDSHIP IS THE PRIMARY VEHICLE
FOR BRINGING A PERSON TO CHRIST

Jesus was described by His peers as a friend of sinners. He intentionally went to them to build relationships with them. Although the religious leaders of the day despised Him for it, Jesus knew it was crucial for success in evangelism. The situation is no different today.

People are the vehicle for carrying the good news into the world. When Jesus called us to be the salt of the earth He did not mean bumper stickers would do the job. Being the light set on a hill does not mean we can rely on radio or TV to broadcast the good news and point the way. It is people who live in the midst of a lost and needy world who carry the message of hope. Those who know us, whom we live with and work with, have been placed within our "Jerusalem." Our relationship with them is the bridge across which Christ can walk.

As was said earlier, an "everyman" approach to evangelism means planning ways to reach every man at every point in his decision-making process. The importance of relationship in this process cannot be overstated. In a relationship there is flexibility to address the need of the moment. In a relationship there is natural follow-up and the sensitivity to sense appropriate timing. Building relationships with unchurched friends is something anyone can learn to do.

With these principles in mind, we now move to practical matters of evangelism. How can we create methods that might work for "everyman"? How can we mobilize the Body of Christ for evangelism? Is it possible to remove the bad taste and inject real joy into the process? Can we find ways to make sharing the good news feel like good news?

Notes

1. Reginald Bibby, "Beyond Circulating the Saints," *Faith Today,* March-April 1990, p. 23.

2. For an excellent discussion of this decision-making process see *What's Gone Wrong with the Harvest,* by James Engel and Wilbert Norton (Grand Rapids: Zondervan, 1981).

15

MOBILIZING FOR EVANGELISM

The Gospel is news to each generation, and we must seek new ways to address our times.
—R. C. Sproul

Imagine, if you will, a "typical" non-Christian. He works an average job, has a wife, two beautiful children, a dog named Fang, and many of the material things common to the rest of us. How is he going to be reached for Christ? He doesn't watch religious TV programs—unless to laugh. He is not moved to repentance by "Christian" bumper stickers. As a rule, he only goes to church for weddings and funerals, although he may think about it at Christmastime. His view of Christianity is that Jesus was probably a great man, but modern churches and preachers are only interested in money.

How will God break through to him so that he will listen? The answer is almost certainly through a relationship with a Christian friend. Hopefully there is a believer in his life who might build a bridge to this man for Christ to walk across. With that knowledge, the process of evangelism becomes exciting and workable. The initial step to reach a non-Christian is simply to build a relationship with him. Anyone can do that!

Once a friendship is begun, there will be opportunities to begin discussing the church, Christ, and the needs of this unbelieving friend. Clearly, every Christian has a different level of skill when it comes to verbalizing his or her faith or answering another person's questions. But everyone can share his or her experience, and everyone can invite someone to a special event where others can help plant more seeds. It is always healthy to bring a non-Christian into contact with other believers. No matter how skilled someone may be in sharing the gospel there is always a need to continue cultivating the seeds that have been planted. The non-Christian's exposure to other believers leads to natural follow-up conversations later.

By creating special events designed to expose non-Christians to Christ in a positive way, any Christian can get involved aggressively in evangelism. This approach also takes into account the fact that most people who do not know Christ need time and repeated exposure if they are to make such a radical decision.

CULTURALLY SENSITIVE STRATEGIES FOR OUTREACH

R. C. Sproul's statement quoted at the beginning of this chapter recognizes the need to present the gospel in fresh ways as faced by every generation. We need to understand our times and so communicate in a way in which people today will understand. Never will that mean altering the message, but it will mean wrapping it in fresh wineskins. For this reason it is helpful to examine culturally sensitive strategies for outreach. (The words *outreach* and *evangelism* are used somewhat synonymously here.)

This section is responding to two significant convictions that every leader who desires to mobilize the body for evangelism must keep clearly in mind. First, the typical Christian does not believe God could use him to lead a non-Christian friend to Christ. Though he may wish otherwise, this pervasive feeling cannot be denied. Christians are afraid of entering conversations about the gospel. They are afraid of failing their God and their friends. Probably most have either given up thinking about it, or they harbor significant guilt over their lack of effectiveness. The fact is most believers shy away from discussion of evangelism and do not believe they could ever be effective in reaching another person. Therefore any effective strategy must assist people in reaching their friends.

The second assumption directly affects our corporate efforts and may bring immediate encouragement to those plagued by the effects of the first assumption. God's intention is that evangelism be a team effort, not conducted by Lone Rangers. Throughout the New Testament the Body of Christ is referred to as a interdependent force. The varieties of gifts, abilities, and interests of God's people are intended to complement and support one another. The process of evangelism is no exception. Call it a team sport if you'd like a catchy title. But God's design is that we learn to assist and encourage one another actively in outreach just as in any other area. By assisting one another we remove the pressure and fear of failure that most people feel.

USING SPECIAL OUTREACH EVENTS

An outreach event—one designed to help people reach their friends—may take on an endless number of forms, but there are two important constants. First, it must be the kind of event to which people in your ministry are willing to bring their non-Christian friends. Second, it must be designed to expose a non-Christian to Christ and to Christians in a positive way so that he or she would be drawn closer to Christ or even receive Him.

Many have found that building special events around common interests can be a great tool. For instance, if a number of men have friends who play golf, organize a golf tournament. Perhaps a breakfast beforehand or an awards banquet afterward would provide the chance for someone to share a personal testimony. In similar fashion, outreach events could be built around tennis, fashions, baseball games, father-son or mother-daughter events. The list of possibilities is endless. The operative principle is simply what kind of events would people be willing to bring their non-Christian friends to?

Another variation on that idea is an event planned around a special theme or need. Some churches have found that a financial seminar fits that mold. Others have designed programs that minister to the needs of single moms. Again, the task of those in leadership is to discover what people would want to bring non-Christian friends to.

For outreach events to be most effective, a few principles of planning have proved to be beneficial.

Be regular. Begin to hold outreach events at regular intervals. As your people begin to own the idea of reaching out to their friends it can be discouraging if another opportunity is months away.

Go all out. Invest as much time, money, and energy as you can into making an outreach effort as good as possible. You will find that the higher the quality, the better your credibility. People have a tendency to evaluate our commitment in light of the intensity of our efforts. The only restriction is that you don't want to blow all of your resources on one event so that everything else for the next six months is mediocre in comparison.

Plan many ingredients. The more aspects you have to your plan the better your chances for a success. When an event is completely depending on one ingredient, what happens if something goes wrong with that item? Use your creativity to add elements that will increase the fun factor. Say, for instance, you are having a father-son fishing trip, why not have someone go along with a video camera, and then hold a dinner at the end of the day. At the dinner the video could add a degree of pure fun, and while you are there it would work easily for someone to share his testimony.

Keep non-Christians in mind. We are used to planning everything with the committed believer in mind, but Jesus would never do that. We must do things with sensitivity and compassion for the secular person. Keeping the non-Christian in mind means avoiding those activities that would clearly make him or her feel out of place. For instance, you probably do not want to break into small groups for thirty minutes of conversational prayer in the middle of an outreach event. If planning events designed to support the process of evangelism is new to you, you will find it a challenge to truly gear things for the unchurched.

PLANNING A SERVICE FOR SEEKERS

In the past few years a number of churches across the country have begun to implement a plan that combines many of the above ingredients on a weekly basis. They have designed a weekly Saturday or Sunday service with the unbeliever in mind.[1] Typical elements of the service might include music, drama, and a message specifically designed to bring God's truth to bear on regular issues of life.

Think about the Christian who has built a relationship with an unbeliever and has begun sharing Christ with him. At a certain point it would be helpful for him to bring this non-Christian friend to a nonthreatening service where God and His Word are presented in relevant ways. The person who has lived thirty, forty, fifty, or more years apart from Christ needs time and input to come to grips with what new life in Christ is all about. A service at a church in which he or she can seek the Lord in comfort can help that process.

Variations on the weekly seeker's service have been tried by some ministries. Every couple of months two or three Sundays in a row are especially designed for nonbelieving friends. There are certain pros and cons to the irregularity of this approach. Obviously it will not work everywhere. However, as a person moves from spiritual apathy to the point of curiosity he may be willing to attend a church service. As he begins to seek God, it is important that we have a place where he can come.

CAUTIONS

As you begin working to mobilize your ministry for evangelism there are a few cautions to be careful of.

NEGLECTING EVANGELISM UNTIL EVERYONE IS READY

Jesus was always involved in personal evangelism. Don't wait until your whole ministry is ready to begin regular, big-event outreach. Personally set the pace by building bridges to non-Christians yourself. As you are able to identify and begin training a ministry team as you start you will want to begin moving into outreach even if only for periodic events.

IGNORING "THE FORTRESS" MENTALITY

In many churches people have become comfortable with the idea that the services and other ministries are really for them, the regular attenders. They view church and its ministries as a safe haven in the midst of a hostile world. This perspective means that there can be significant resistance to adding or altering programs in order to reach non-Christians. It's not that non-Christians are the enemy, but if they begin coming, things in the church will change.

Please understand, the need is for those who lead to be prepared to deal sensitively with those who feel their church being threatened. Love them. Pray for them. Be patient with them. Model a love for lost people in your own life. And give God room to do His own work in believers' lives.

GIVING UP AFTER A SHORT TIME

When a ministry begins moving out aggressively into evangelism it is moving directly into the enemy's territory. As a result, it is not uncommon for discouragements or battles in other areas to creep up. It is also true that things often begin slowly. Do not give up when your efforts don't show the results

you expected as quickly as you expected them. Evaluate, refine, pray, and continue. Ultimately God accepts the responsibility to bring fruit out of the seeds that are planted. Our
responsibility is to remain faithful.

The greatest joy of the Christian life is being used by God
—especially in evangelism. Nothing else in all the earth com-
pares to it. God's inexhaustible joy over the reconciliation of
the lost is detailed in the parables of Luke 15. The angels rejoice in heaven over one sinner who is saved (Luke 15:10). On
earth, those who participate in the process of redemption participate in the resulting joy as well. In mobilizing for evangelism
—in addition to carrying out God's plan—you are tangibly creating a means for people to discover the depth of God's joy.

Note

1. Bill Hybels and Willow Creek Community Church have done an excellent job in identifying the nonbeliever. They have been forerunners in fashioning a service for
seekers. Write to their Seeds Tape ministry to order a tape of their philosophy of
ministry. It is an excellent resource. Willow Creek Community Church; 67 East
Algonquin Road; South Barrington, Illinois 60010.

PHASE 4

RESTRUCTURING FOR MULTIPLICATION

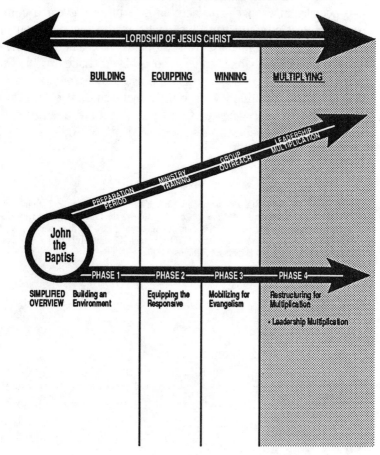

16

LEADERSHIP MULTIPLICATION

*Here is a trustworthy saying: If anyone sets his heart
on being an overseer, he desires a noble task.*
—1 Timothy 3:1

There he was, the man of the decade—no, make that the
man of the century. Quite possibly he was the greatest
leader of all time. Nonetheless, he was burning himself out.
From the first moments of daybreak until long past sunset, he
was consumed with the demands of his job. The massive responsibilities of leadership were compounded by continual con-
flicts among his people. Daily he was buried by the need to
resolve petty disputes, adjudicate legal matters, and respond to
chronic complaining, not to mention providing desperately
needed direction for his people. He had never worked harder.
Yet he could never get it all done.

Thank the Lord for fathers-in-law at a time like this. Jethro was able to get Moses to listen and face his problem head-
on. Simply stated, Moses was trying to do everything himself.
He needed to spread the load among others. Jethro made him
face the fact that he could never do everything by himself. And
neither can we!

Have we learned this lesson? In all honesty, are we fully
convinced of the need to share leadership responsibilities with
others? Our egos might enjoy the belief that we alone are qualified or chosen to carry out the work of the ministry. However,

if we allow ourselves to believe or even to act as if everything depends upon us we are making the same mistake Moses did. Worse, we are denying a central truth about God's design for His church. God has called leaders to equip others to also become leaders (Eph. 4:11-13). God has not called us to operate as Lone Rangers!

THE PRIORITY OF A TEAM APPROACH

As Christ's ministry grew, it became necessary to train and appoint others to shepherd segments of the ministry. Jesus knew He could not adequately meet the needs of everyone Himself, so He began to entrust some of the responsibilities to His disciples. That was necessary to allow for the continued growth and development of His disciples, and it was necessary as the final step of building a ministry that would continue expanding in a healthy manner.

In our day of mega-churches and personality-based leadership it is easy to miss the importance of a team approach. A misplaced hunger for success can easily cause a leader to think he must do it all. Yet the pattern of Christ, the nature of the Body of Christ, and the demands of ministry all say differently. Our plan must be to nurture and appoint leaders who will be shepherds over segments of the ministry.

This raises an important issue which must be addressed before we go any further. What exactly do we mean by the term "leader"? Unfortunately, in today's church we often use the term loosely. Nearly every conference, seminar, or retreat is labeled as a leadership retreat. Nearly everyone who does anything in the church is referred to as a leader. This overly general use of the term "leader" clouds the important focus of leadership multiplication.

More than a definition of terms is at stake here. At issue is the fundamental concept of what people are being raised up and appointed to do. Leaders, in the sense used here, are those who have been given responsibility for a segment of the ministry. Perhaps a better term is "shepherd." Any given ministry will likely have only a few shepherds. Most of those casually referred to as leaders are really "workers" who serve the ministry and would rightfully be a part of ministry training. A shepherd, or leader, is a worker who has proved himself faithful and able in serving others and is now responsible to oversee and shepherd a segment of the flock. A New Testament corollary would be the term "elder."[1]

Rather than casually using the label "leader" we need to realize that it represents a position not to be taken lightly. Each leader works with the people under his care to carry out the ministry of winning, building, and equipping people. If this increased responsibility is not sobering enough, remember that leaders also face more stringent judgment (James 3:1). A stricter use of the term "leader" reflects the magnitude of that role.

THE LEADERSHIP TRAINING PHASE OF JESUS' MINISTRY

Whereas Christ's desire was to reach the masses, the genius and risk of His strategy was the priority of investing in the twelve. He spent 100 percent of His time with them—training them, teaching them, investing in them. It was a risk, but it was calculated. It was God's method! It is in this leadership appointment phase that the true genius of Christ's strategy unfolds most fully.[2]

The twelve had been with Jesus from the beginning. They had come to trust Him as their Messiah. They had been involved with Him in ministry training and outreach. Now they were ready for leadership responsibilities. It was a natural outgrowth—under God's guidance—of their own development. Jesus' investment in these men was not just because He liked them better than everyone else. It was not because they possessed the most natural abilities. His plan was to nurture them and equip them to eventually become leaders within His ministry.

What we see in Jesus Christ is an unequaled communication model. While he reached the multitudes, he was equipping a group of twelve men for an in-depth ministry. And while he was equipping twelve men, he was especially equipping Peter and John for a more foundational ministry that would go beyond even that of the other apostles. This is obvious from the ministry of these two men as revealed in the book of Acts, as well as by the New Testament literature they wrote. It was no secret to the twelve that Jesus Christ had a special ministry for these men and particularly for Peter. The way he singled out Peter for special instructions and lessons verifies this point. [3]

Just as Christ formally appointed the twelve in this phase of His ministry we too must plan to restructure for multiplication. We must allow the leaders God has given us to surface and then restructure our ministry to allow them to learn and begin using their shepherding skills. This restructuring will also affect the one who has been the primary leader until now. At this point the person who has been the sole leader becomes the leader of leaders.

Restructuring for Multiplication

As surprising as it may sound at this point, leadership training and appointment does not mean starting something brand new in your ministry. It is simply multiplying the number of people who are guiding segments of the ministry in the winning-building-equipping process. Whereas up to this point a ministry may have all fallen under the care of one shepherd, now there are others as well. Where originally there was one leader, that person is now a leader of leaders. Look at the following diagram for a graphic illustration of how this development occurs.

The point is that restructuring *must* happen, or the ministry will peak out at a certain size and stop growing because needs will not be met. Failure to restructure will also result in the loss of potential leaders because they will have no way to

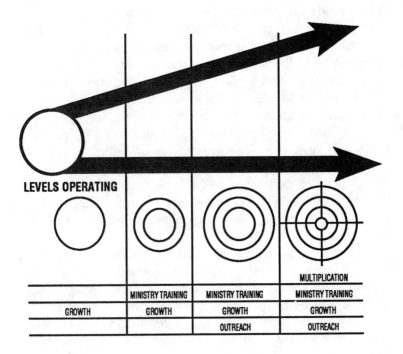

LEVELS OPERATING

			MULTIPLICATION
	MINISTRY TRAINING	MINISTRY TRAINING	MINISTRY TRAINING
GROWTH	GROWTH	GROWTH	GROWTH
		OUTREACH	OUTREACH

develop their gifts for ministry if there is no place for them to be used.

This does not mean that a ministry is incomplete without multiple leaders. The first three phases of ministry development—building a foundation, equipping the team, and reaching the masses—cover the whole spectrum of the Great Commission. However, leadership multiplication is needed to guide a ministry beyond the limits of one person's ability or energy.

Practically, multiplication means that segments within the church are able to take off. For example, a leader of a college ministry will be building a foundation for growth, equipping people for ministry, and then attempting to reach other college students with them. A high school ministry or singles ministry or any other area of ministry within the church will seek to do the same. In some cases even adult Sunday school classes could seek to build a fully balanced ministry this way. The possibilities are limited only by the number of leaders available to shepherd those areas.

Effective leadership multiplication will yield the exciting result of continual ministry expansion. There will be a growing movement of leaders, workers, new Christians, and curiosity seekers. As the ministry is developing, one person probably oversees the development of each level, or phase. But when you begin appointing other leaders over different segments of the ministry, you may see geometric expansion—both in quality and in quantity.

FINDING AND TRAINING SHEPHERDS

Our human tendency is to view the leadership role as the pinnacle of spirituality, but that is simply not the case. A fully trained disciple has learned to reach his or her peers and is active in doing so. He may continue to grow and become more consistent and dependable, but leadership is not the next step for everyone. Leaders are appointed to oversee people and the ministry structure. Different qualities and spiritual gifts are im-

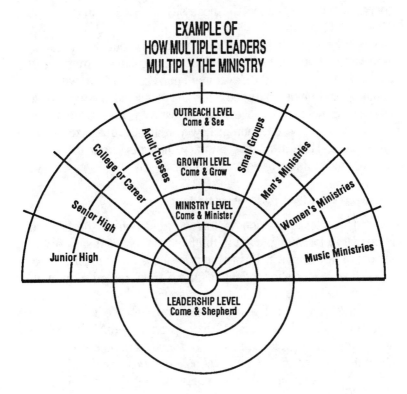

EXAMPLE OF HOW MULTIPLE LEADERS MULTIPLY THE MINISTRY

OUTREACH LEVEL
Come & See

GROWTH LEVEL
Come & Grow

MINISTRY LEVEL
Come & Minister

LEADERSHIP LEVEL
Come & Shepherd

Junior High

Senior High

College or Career

Adult Classes

Small Groups

Men's Ministries

Women's Ministries

Music Ministries

portant at different times. There are time constraints and other concerns, not to mention the necessity of God's leading in the selection of leaders.

At the same time, leaders do not come out of a vacuum. You watch for them to grow out of the regular environment of the ministry. A rightly developed ministry that is winning, building, and equipping people for Christ should produce those who could be leaders over the ministry. However, that still doesn't answer the question of how you are to recognize potential leaders. Here are a few primary thoughts about the selection and the training of potential leaders.

LOOK FOR DEMONSTRATED FAITHFULNESS

In view of the serious nature of a position as shepherd, it is crucial to look for proved faithfulness. When Paul says not to appoint a new convert, this is the point he is making. The life of a potential leader should demonstrate a track record of growth, ministry, and spiritual faithfulness in general.

Each of the qualities necessary in one who is ready for ministry training (see chap. 12) is important here. Perhaps the key difference at this point is the added commodity of time. Over the span of time a leader should demonstrate faithfulness, availability, teachability, and enthusiasm. His character by now has been tested and proved trustworthy.

Perfection is not the goal, but neither is mediocre spirituality acceptable. A leader in the ministry has significant influence, which can be misused to damage the cause of Christ and individual lives of people. Wise stewardship means appointing leaders who have shown themselves faithful.

LOOK FOR MATURE MINISTRY

Imagine you are flying somewhere on business. After going through his preflight routine the pilot pulls the plane out onto the taxiway. As you wait in line to take off, he welcomes the passengers and announces that this is his first flight—not just his first flight for this airline, but his first ever. "Don't worry," he says, "I have a whole pile of books here, including navigational aids. I'm a quick learner, so you will all be fine."

Of course the story is absurd. Why? Because in our day pilots train incessantly. They fly simulators, they fly with trainers, they study, and they are never allowed in the pilot's seat without experience. Most airlines only hire experienced pilots, then train them further, matching them with more experienced pilots, and even have observers fly with newer pilots.

In appointing leaders we are doing the equivalent of choosing the pilots who will train, nurture, and guide other pilots. We are selecting individuals to direct the course of the ministry and care for the people along the way. It is important that they be familiar with the territory.

A leader can authentically take his people only where he has gone already. For this reason leaders should be able and active in ministry among their peers. Those who are leaders, who are responsible for a segment of the ministry need to set the pace and give direction to all phases of the ministry under their care.

Although it may have appeared arbitrary to divide the ministry training process into seven stages (see chap. 11), those divisions become very important at this point. A person who could be considered for a position as leader has grown to the M7 level. He has learned to minister in many areas and has the personal practice of strategizing and working to penetrate his sphere of influence.

Another way to recognize maturity in ministry is that quite often the person capable of being a leader is already doing the work of a shepherd. He has probably seen people come to Christ. He may be actively equipping others for ministry and nurturing them. It is common for the leaders whom God taps to already have shepherding responsibilities of some kind. This is a good indicator of a calling in a full- or part-time staff member as well as a lay leader.

KEEP UP THE GOOD WORK

None of us will ever finish growing in our ability to do the work of the ministry. The ministry training process lasts a lifetime. Therefore when leaders are appointed they don't abandon the practices and priorities of the past. On the contrary, they keep pursuing the same plans for growth.

Leaders will always need to grow in the six foundational areas discussed in phase one—building. They will always need to sharpen their skills in the areas of ministry detailed in phase two—equipping. And they will never exhaust the areas of growth in outreach—phase three. To this end the one who is a leader of leaders invests himself in the lives of his other leaders.

After Jesus formally appointed the twelve He invested just as much if not more time with them. You can see the fruit of this investment in the quantity of material recorded in the gospels devoted to the latter part of His ministry. Much of this material would have been the subject of Jesus' special training and encouragement for these leaders.

LEADERS ARE APPOINTED

Jesus prayed for workers, but He carefully appointed leaders. The difference is important. Leaders as have been defined here could not be found via a "help wanted" ad. Can you imagine a bulletin announcement calling for volunteers to be one of Jesus' twelve disciples?

Jesus' method involved time with these men to observe their lives, and it involved the discernment found only through prayer. The same pattern would serve our ministries well. Look for those who have demonstrated faithfulness in every area and have grown to maturity in ministry. Bathe the process in prayer, and appoint leaders as God directs you.

POTENTIAL PITFALLS

As you enter this phase of ministry there are a few problems to guard against. By quickly looking at these problems you will not only be prepared, but they will provide a fresh perspective on a few other critical issues.

APPOINTING LEADERS AT THE WRONG TIME

Scripture warns against the laying on of hands too quickly (1 Tim. 5:22). In our zeal it is easy to jump the gun and appoint a person who is not ready. An immature person can destroy a segment of the ministry. Leadership that does not have M7 convictions can quickly move a church or ministry away from M7 priorities. Whereas most people believe in the importance of M7 priorities, leaders must have nonnegotiable convictions about them. It is too easy to allow a church or ministry degenerate to only M1-M3 priorities under pressure. We then lose sight of our highest purposes. On the other hand, waiting too long to appoint leaders can retard growth. Saturate these steps with prayer, and be willing to do whatever God directs—whether it is wait or go.

SPENDING TOO LITTLE TIME WITH YOUR LEADERSHIP

You cannot be with your leadership team too much. As a matter of fact, part of the restructuring that occurs at this stage is a rearrangement of time on the part of the main leader. The focus of time is on multiplying the ministry through the quality work of other leaders. To that end it would not be inappropriate for about 45 percent of the leader's time to be spent with his other leaders. (A suggested formula for a leader's time usage is 45 percent with other leaders, 15 percent in ministry training activities, 15 percent in growth level activities, 15 percent in outreach activities, and 10 percent in prayer.) Unfortunately it is not uncommon for leaders to be appointed and then abandoned. Look to the model of Christ for encouragement in this area. He carefully invested Himself in the twelve, yet He did so without ignoring other needs and opportunities.

LISTENING TOO MUCH TO OUR CULTURE

Our culture measures success by educational degrees, statistical gains, big buildings, and hefty bank accounts. God measures success by changed lives and leaders who are producing them. Guard yourself against using the world's standards to select leaders. In the ongoing work of encouragement and evaluation be careful that neither you nor your other leaders begin to evaluate progress by the world's measure.

NOT ALLOWING NEW LEADERS TO DEVELOP

Failure to continually restructure to allow additional leaders to develop will result in losing leaders and stagnation of the ministry. The search for leaders is continual. In fact, the multiplication process intended by the methods of Christ suggests that each leader constantly looks for other leaders to be trained. As leaders produce and nurture more leaders the ministry grows in its ability to meet needs and carry the gospel.

The leader's primary task in this phase is to help new shepherds define their roles and accomplish their tasks. He does not, however, remove himself from ministry to others. Where Christ's strategy was to reach the masses we see the genius in His plan of multiplication at this level. He targeted the masses by investing in the twelve.

His methods are easy to comprehend. As we follow His strategy and appoint leaders who can multiply the ministry, we have the chance to participate in the work of the Great Commission in a powerful way.

Notes

1. This is not to be entangled with church government structures. The issue is one of ministry, not title. Key passages include: 2 Timothy 2:2; 1 Peter 5:3; Titus 1:5-6.

2. Refer to the comments in chapter 3, quoted from Robert E. Coleman's *The Master Plan of Evangelism.*

3. Gene Getz, *Sharpening the Focus of the Church* (Chicago: Moody, 1974), pp. 168-69.

SECTION 3

PRINCIPLES FOR THE LONG HAUL

"PASTOR, WHAT DO YOU MEAN OUR CHURCH IS NOT GROWING BECAUSE WE ARE SET IN OUR WAYS?"

17

CULTIVATING VISION

The saddest thing in the world is people who can see, but have no vision.

—Helen Keller

Those poignant words of Helen Keller hit home. Lack of vision or purpose afflicts many people. Mired in the demands and wearisome duties of the moment, we experience a gnawing sense of meaninglessness. Somehow when vision is lost, even the noblest of ventures becomes just another task to be completed.

Vision is that compelling conviction which determines where you are headed. It is that tangible expression of purpose which ignites your passion for progress. Spiritual vision is a handle on the desires God has for your life. Clear vision provides the ability to walk in the present while picturing where you are headed. It defines direction for life and ministry. Without a sense of vision the routine of daily life can easily fog your sense of significance and direction. Vision enables you to keep the whole forest in mind even while focused on a single tree.

Sadly, when there is lack of vision in the church even the work of the kingdom can become mundane. Sunday school teachers begin to loathe the day they agreed to help out with those squirrelly sixth-grade boys. Bible study leaders cannot forget the fact that this year's Bible study material is not what they would have chosen. Ushers, choir members, and committee members become more consumed with getting out of work than with how they can contribute. Without vision, a sense of true significance is hard to maintain.

Clearly communicated vision is one of those far-reaching, life-giving ingredients of a ministry geared for the long haul. New programs quickly become old. Flashy ideas of today carry less razzle-dazzle tomorrow. But clear compelling vision continually re-invigorates the efforts of any ministry.

Dangers of Lack of Vision

Sometimes it is easier to understand how important something is by looking at what fills the vacuum of its absence. Perhaps one of the best ways to help you see what vision can do is to examine what happens without it. Here are some potential dangers that can result from a lack of vision.

A PASSIVE "ME-ISTIC," OR "ENTERTAIN ME," MIND-SET

One of the first symptoms to appear in the absence of vision is a lost sense of calling. An "entertain me" mind-set replaces an intensity of purpose. Activities and programs are viewed through eyes only concerned with "What's in it for me?" Those in positions of leadership soon feel they are spinning their wheels. This maintenance mind-set can easily create an underlying apathy where there ought to be a contagious, dynamic zeal for changed lives.

BITTER FEUDS OVER NEEDED CHANGE

Following closely on the heels of the "entertain me" attitude are often painful confrontations over even the smallest changes. Granted, change is always scary to some degree. Some people are seriously unsettled by the unknown prospects of change, and the wise leader is sensitive to that. But there is often a caustic element of resistance when change is not connected to vision. Fierce battles erupt in congregational meetings and behind closed doors. Whether the issue is as simple as the color of the nursery carpet or as complex as the need for an additional staff member matters little. In the absence of vision people evaluate change on the basis of personal preference alone. Most unfortunate is the fact that serious and often permanent scars are formed by this unnecessary conflict. Clear and driving vision cannot prevent all conflict, but it can put necessary change in perspective.

UNWISE DECISIONS THAT AFFECT PROGRAMS

We live in a day where tremendous options and resources for effective ministry programming are available. Every day our faithful postal service delivers enticements to try out one type of program or another. Choices must be made even while sorting the mail. We must also face the fact that there are unlimited needs to be met. Those in leadership must continually select which needs their ministry can address. Choices not only have to be made but explained to affected parties. Without a sense of vision and direction, how does a person make the choices necessary? Clear vision provides a primary filter for making the necessary decisions of ministry leadership.

INACCURATE EVALUATION

It is possible to evaluate specific events but impossible to evaluate progress without knowing where you are heading. Without vision, without a clearly understood target, how can a ministry know how they are doing? Without vision, fruitfulness can only be measured in terms of efficiency and quantity. For example, "Did things run smoother this year?" "Did more people come than last time?" "Did we do better financially?"

LOST LEADERS

Without direction, those who have grown to become leaders easily become bored and unchallenged. They don't think their labor is connected to a purpose. In some people the result of this frustration can be an apathy and disillusionment about ministry. At other times leaders who feel unchallenged or bored simply leave for another ministry. In either case, without vision you run the risk of losing leaders—either bodily or functionally. Leaders need to be challenged, but they need to be challenged by vision.

Perhaps a look at these dangers from a totally different angle might prove helpful. Imagine you and your family have decided to take your dream vacation. You will be traveling from the Midwest to the sun, surf, and glitter of southern California. Although you would love to fly there, the prohibitive cost leads you to take the adventurous approach—you will drive.

Day one gets off to a good start. The three kids are busy talking about all they will do at Disneyland, the beach, Universal Studios, and Yosemite. The two of you in the front seat relax a little, now that you are finally out of the house. Naive as it may be, you harbor the notion that this trip might be more pleasant and the kids less cantankerous than usual.

Sooner or later, however, certain predictable things begin to happen. The kids' toys begin to break or get lost under the seat. Little Suzy has to use the bathroom—for the eighteenth time. Junior gets his gum stuck in Betsy's hair. And Dad's blood pressure is rising with every increased decibel of noise. You haven't been gone two days, and the happy little campers have become replaced by crabby, fidgety, fussbudgets, bent on making you miserable.

What keeps you going at moments like those? When the family car is traveling through hot and desolate stretches of road where even fast food sounds delightful, what produces hope? The answer is found in the clear vision of where you are heading. It is that picture of what lies ahead that keeps everyone going. It is also the commitment to that vision that keeps you from becoming sidetracked.

Traveling down the highway you face an incessant barrage of billboard advertisements. Whether they describe some classic "tourist trap" or a legitimate point of interest, you must constantly address the impact such a diversion would make on the rest of your vacation. If your dream is to spend two weeks in southern California, then you cannot afford to fritter your time away along the road.

"Wild Willy's Water Park and Moccasin Store" might be a great place to spend an afternoon on other occasions. However, if spending half a day there now means you will miss a day at the beach, you may not want to pay that price. It is your desire for a great vacation in California that keeps you going and helps you make difficult decisions along the way. Without clear focus motivating such a trip, it would be nearly impossible to deal with the tensions that arise.

The same things happen in ministry. Regardless of good beginnings, there will be difficult days. There will be decisions with long-range implications. There will be choices between two or more good options. There will be moments of exhaustion when everyone would just prefer to take off. Just as in the family cross-country trip, clear vision will provide the impetus to keep moving when the going gets tough. It will keep people focused on the value of their contribution. Clear vision will also help you evaluate and be encouraged by your progress, as well.

COMPONENTS OF HEALTHY VISION

Hopefully you are sold on the virtues of well-defined vision for ministry. In all likelihood, you have experienced the results of its presence or absence. What are the components of a healthy vision? As you develop a statement of vision to guide your ministry the following four components are essential.

1. SHOULD REFLECT GREAT COMMISSION PRIORITIES

At first glance this principle may seem obvious. Yet in the process of defining vision, it is important to keep from becoming distracted by good but nonessential ideas. For instance, "God has called us to provide the best potluck suppers in town," might be a tasty idea but probably would not meet Great Commission criteria. Your objective must be to discern God's vision for your ministry. His desire will always be consistent with Scripture, so push yourself to address Great Commission priorities.

2. SHOULD BE SPECIFICALLY DESIGNED FOR YOUR MINISTRY

Obviously when everyone begins with a limited set of biblical priorities there should be great similarity in the vision for different ministries. Yet that does not mean God has called every ministry to do the same thing in the same way. A healthy vision statement should reflect the personality of your ministry, your target community, and the unique passions and gifts of those in leadership. Your vision statement should be consistent with God's reason for calling you into existence—at this time, in this location, with the particular opportunities you have available.

3. SHOULD BE COMPELLING, PASSIONATE, AND WITHOUT "RELIGIOUS TECHNOSPEAK"

Flowery, theological, two-dollar words may sound impressive to some, but they will not accomplish the goal of communicating vision. The vision God has given your ministry should be stated in "everyman" terms. There is no need to say, "By the ordination of our omnipotent King, this ecclesiastical expression has been predestined to carry the oracle of divine reconciliation to our spiritually depraved and deprived peers." Such complexity does not touch people's hearts, nor will it move them to action. Rather you should simply say, "God has called this church to bring the good news to our lost and needy neighborhood." Healthy vision is best defined in terms that get right to the heart of the matter. The best words are those that regular people understand.

4. SHOULD BE TRANSFERABLE

Until this point it has been implied, although not explicitly stated, that you should seek to capture your vision in written from. In fact, you should consider formulating a specific vision statement. Putting your thoughts into a statement of carefully chosen words makes your vision easily transferable. One person can communicate it to another without losing anything in the translation. In this transferable form people can read it, repeat it, and hopefully remember it.

However, to be easily transferable it must be short and memorable. Your task is to capture your passion for ministry in a single short statement. You don't want to sacrifice content, but work to communicate fully in as few words as possible.

DEVELOPING A VISION STATEMENT

Whether you are at the helm of a ministry, part of a leadership team, or you just want to clarify your vision for your own life, the process is the same. The rest of this chapter is devoted to the practical process of developing healthy vision. These next pages are hands-on suggestions and lend themselves to interaction with pen and paper.

You might want to make an appointment with yourself when you will carefully work through this material and crystallize your personal vision. You might also want to suggest to the rest of your ministry leadership that you go away together to work this through. Some of the steps prove to be easier or more helpful for some people than others, and that is perfectly fine. Just pray your way through the questions in each step, and allow the Lord to speak to you as He provides you with the building blocks of a healthy vision.

STEP ONE: REVIEW THE PAST

The process God has used to bring you to this point has not been coincidental. Specific circumstances, relationships, and biblical passages have probably forged your convictions and desires. Taking time to review those important influences will rekindle your confidence in God's leading. It may also help you reawaken those motivating factors which have contributed to your passions for ministry.

Questions to ask yourself:

"What are some ways I have seen God work in my life in the past?"

"What has happened in my life to give me a desire to be used as a leader in ministry?"

"Has God used any particular person to teach me and motivate me to work with others?"

"What lessons did I learn from that person?"

STEP TWO: IDENTIFY BIBLICAL PRIORITIES

This step does not mean that you need to search for some never-before-unearthed biblical principles. But because healthy vision needs to reflect Great Commission priorities, the discipline of identifying them provides a needed focus.

Ask yourself these questions:

"What major priorities did Christ give to His disciples?"

"What passages has God used to refocus my attention on His agenda for the church?"

"What passages has God used to stir my passions for the work of Christ?"

"Am I aware of any common desires for the ministry of the church that are *not* major priorities in Scripture?"

"If I were forced to choose one priority of Scripture to stand out above all the other options, which would it be?"

STEP THREE: VERBALIZE PRESENT PASSIONS AND OPPORTUNITIES

Look around at the potential in your ministry. Most likely, there are opportunities or needs that stand out to you. Perhaps there are certain kinds of ministry or certain kinds of people that you are very passionate about. It is possible that those areas reflect a burden God has nurtured within you. (This is true for individuals as well as entire ministries.) Verbalizing those things about which God has made you especially sensitive can give additional insight into what He has called you to.

Wrestle with these questions:

"What opportunities for ministry do I feel strongly about?"

"What needs am I, as a church or individually, in a unique position to meet?"

"What single words represent the aspects of ministry I feel most strongly about?"

STEP FOUR: IDENTIFY FUTURE HOPES AND DREAMS

Now try looking ahead. God's work in the past has prepared you for the present, but He is also preparing you for future ministry. God's desires for the future are probably more intense, more incredible, and perhaps more scary than any we could dream of ourselves. However, in defining vision it is important to take off the blinders in order to identify the hopes and dreams God has given you. Allow the Holy Spirit to expand your thoughts about the future.

Here are some questions that might help:

"In my wildest dreams, what would I want to see God do in our ministry in the next few years?"

"How do I think our ministry would be different in five years if God could have His way totally unhindered?"

"If God were to give me a blank check so that I had unlimited time, energy, and resources, what would I love to see Him do in and through our ministry?"

STEP FIVE: PUT IT ALL TOGETHER

This final step is simultaneously simple and very difficult. Some people find the brainstorming processes of the first four steps easy, yet they struggle greatly at this point. Others feel as if they have already endured a strenuous workout by now and find the consolidation process fairly obvious. Whatever the case, you have now rounded third base and are heading for home.

Don't panic! A vision statement does not need to include reference to nor the implications of every thought generated above. Instead of trying to include everything, you now want to look for a common theme or two that recurred frequently. Perhaps you found that your response to one particular question said it all for you. At the same time, if nothing seems to stand out, ask the Lord to make things clear. Look for a common thread to be woven throughout your answers. Give God time, and He will make His way clear to you.

In a nutshell the question to ask at this point is this: *Having thought about it many different ways, what is the vision God has given me/us for ministry?*

VISION, GOALS, AND PROGRAMS

There is one other potential roadblock to this process. It is the confusion over the difference between vision, goals, and programs. If you find yourself still struggling with the specifics of what should go into your vision statement, this confusion may be the problem.

For some reason most of us are more comfortable talking about the tangible and the immediate than the long-range or the ideal. In the church that means we are prone to discuss programs more than goals and goals more than vision. To make matters worse, when vision or goals are being tackled by a group, there is always a tendency to gravitate back to programs.

All three are important. In fact, all three are directly related. But all three are distinct, and each holds a different and essential purpose.

> **Vision:** The big picture. Defines direction. Vision clarifies where we are heading, what God desires for us.

Goals:	Short-term steps. Move us in the direction of our vision. They are measurable targets, intermediate steps.
Programs:	Activities designed to achieve goals. Programs are the arena where the hands-on work and the progress toward goals and vision takes place.

As you clarify your vision statement you will want to be sure that it paints the big picture, the direction for your ministry (and possibly your own life). It should not be a measurable achievement—that would be a goal. And it should avoid any reference to a program. On the other hand, the programs of your ministry should be able to see how they contribute to the pursuit of your vision.

ONE MORE THING—COMMUNICATE IT!

Once you have developed your vision statement you are ready to communicate it. In fact, communicating it will be your greatest challenge. To put it bluntly, *make it your agenda to communicate your vision to everyone and anyone, at every opportunity, in every possible way.*

You should set a personal priority of becoming the champion of the vision of your ministry. Unfortunately we are all good at tossing the ball into someone else's lap, but your vision will be lost through simple attrition if you do that. Instead, use every possible medium and every possible opportunity to tell everyone who will listen about the work God has called you to. Picture yourself running a flag up a flagpole and flying it in full view of everyone. You want everyone to own the vision that guides your ministry. To make that happen you will need to keep it before them.

18

THE ART OF CHALLENGING

You can lead a horse to water, but you cannot make him drink. . . . However, a little salt in his oats goes a long, long way.

John had been the pastor of his church for about two and a half years. He went there directly out of seminary to work with a small group of believers who had begun a new church. By all measurements, things had gone smoothly and successfully during the past thirty months. But now John was questioning his effectiveness as a leader and even his call to the ministry.

It all started with a special seminar he attended. Like any good leader, John periodically took time to evaluate his ministry and the needs of his people. Over time he began to realize the need to be more intentional about helping them grow spiritually. Mere attendance at corporate events was not facilitating the growth and stability they needed. *This upcoming seminar on small group ministries might provide the right solution,* he thought. So John and his wife attended the seminar. They got fired up. Everything seemed so clear. If only they could get small group ministries going, the needed growth and encouragement would take place.

John ordered a set of materials and began to publicize his plan for small group Bible studies. Inserts were put in the bulletins. Announcements were made from the pulpit. John's wife prepared some posters. It appeared that all the details were coming together perfectly. Perfectly, that is, until it came time for people to sign up.

After the publicity had been put in place, people were given two weeks to sign-up. Those who wanted to participate were simply to register in the church lobby. However, the first Sunday came and went without a single person committing to become involved. Caught off guard, but undaunted, John manned the telephone to contact those whom he thought would be interested. "Thanks for the call, but our evenings are so booked up already." "Oh yeah, we've been meaning to talk about it, but just never got around to it . . . we'll let you know next Sunday." "I'm not sure we are ready for the commitment to an every week thing. You won't be offended if we pass this time around will you?" And so went the responses.

By the time registration was finished, only three people had signed up. Three people wouldn't even comprise one healthy group, not to mention the fact that all three apparently signed up because they felt sorry for their pastor. After all, "This program seemed so important to him." The lack of response left John battling a critical spirit. He could barely restrain himself from berating his people for what he perceived to be a lack of spirituality, misaligned priorities, and an obvious lack of appreciation for all his efforts on their behalf. He was discouraged.

Has this—or something like it—ever happened to you? Odds are, somewhere along the way, you have labored to develop programs intended to meet real needs and yet found your labors met with disinterest. This common experience demonstrates the truth of the adage stated above, "You can lead a horse to water, but you can't make him drink." Every ministry leader longs to help people progress to greater levels of maturity. We spot needs to be met, and we seek to meet those needs. Unfortunately, even the best water in the land will not make someone drink. We must learn to stimulate thirst. Learning to stimulate that thirst, that hunger to learn and grow, could be called the art of challenging.

"Challenging" is the process of encouraging, urging, or stimulating someone to pursue a greater level of involvement or commitment. It is the process of discerning where people are and challenging them to take a further step with Christ. Developing this skill—it's an art really—will provide needed direction at many points in your ministry. It will help you personalize the impact of your ministry. Effective challenging is a practice that will make an acute difference over the long haul.

THE NATURE OF EFFECTIVE CHALLENGING

Jesus constantly demonstrated profound insight into where people were spiritually. His discernment formed the platform from which He challenged people to new levels of commitment. For example, Jesus' initial invitation to His disciples was simply to come and see (John 1:39). He did not make it a lengthy treatise on the cost of committed discipleship. Rather, He challenged them to take a first step, to "follow me" (John 1:43; Matt. 9:9). Further down the road He urged them to a greater commitment when He added the challenge to become "fishers of men" (Mark 1:17). Much later He would challenge them to the ultimate level of devotion with the call to take up their cross and follow Him (Luke 14:27, 33).

Jesus challenged each individual in different but consistently appropriate ways. He did not use a cookie cutter approach nor a mere handful of challenges used repetitively. Jesus' intensely personal approach was always designed to challenge people to the next appropriate step of commitment. His example forms the heart of what is meant by challenging: Helping people pursue a greater level of commitment to Christ.

For any of us to effectively challenge people we must consciously assess where they are spiritually. Then we must identify ways to help them take the next step. This assessment, combined with our goal of helping them grow in their commitment to Christ, can produce an extraordinary benefit. The more effective we are at challenging, the more effectively we will learn to specifically connect programs to real needs.

Think about it; when your focus is on challenging people to take the next step of growth in their commitment to Christ, you naturally begin tailoring your programs to make that possible. You will find you are never satisfied to maintain a program that is not focused on a particular need. Your planning process will naturally begin to define the people and needs that are targeted by each program.

Your presentation of ministry and program opportunities will become much more focused as well. Many times churches and other ministries communicate invitations for particular programs as if everyone already felt the need and the benefits of those programs. Bible studies, special services, unique ministry opportunities, and other invaluable efforts for the kingdom are not clearly connected with the needs of people. As a result, members of your congregation view everything as simply another option. That was the problem of John's approach to his small group ministry. Although the program was intended to meet a real need, his people felt no urgency and no personal need to participate.

Effective challenging means helping people connect their needs with an opportunity for spiritual growth. It means helping someone recognize his or her need and consider doing something about it. It is simply not very fruitful to wait on the sidelines hoping that people will automatically understand when and what to do in order to grow in their commitment to Christ.

ELEMENTS OF AN EFFECTIVE CHALLENGE

If you still sense any fogginess over the concept of challenging, a look at the specific elements of an effective challenge should bring things into focus. You will also find that the four primary elements in the challenging process make an excellent outline for discussion among your leadership team. In fact, as you work together with other leaders in your ministry, it would be wise to regularly evaluate your progress in each area.

1. CREATE THIRST

Think back to the case study at the beginning of this chapter. John had made an accurate assessment of the needs of his people. In fact, we might assume that his proposed solution would have been ideal to meet the real need which he knew to exist. However, the people in his church did not feel that need. They had no sense of thirst longing to be satisfied.

In your own life you experience the reality of this principle every day. When you go to your mailbox and retrieve the day's mail, you probably scan it quickly to separate the junk mail from the good stuff. Junk mail is that pile of unasked for paper which fills your mailbox and clutters your kitchen, telling you about things you don't want or need. If, however, you were to receive an ad for something you desperately needed, your response would be quite different. Bottom line—when you feel the need, you pay close attention to anything with the potential to meet that need. It works the same way in the spiritual arena.

The people of your ministry are no less spiritual because they need you to awaken their sense of need. Creating thirst is a normal part of working with people. "Yeah, but if they were really serious about Christ they would be self-motivated." Certainly there is truth to that perspective, but the task every leader in the Body of Christ faces is to help people grow to that point. We cannot let people flounder on their own without helping them along the way. Those in ministry leadership should help people understand their needs for growth and then show them how to meet those needs.

On the practical side, how does one go about creating or awakening a sense of thirst in other people? Although there are many possible ways to do it, none is so singularly effective as the use of good questions. Someone once said, "In challenging people, Jesus asked twice as many questions as He gave answers."[1]

For example, Matthew 11:7-9 shows Jesus using eight questions in three verses as He attempts to answer questions about John the Baptist. Good questions force a person to think. They invite him to make his own conclusions. Questions stimulate evaluation, whereas straight information does not demand response.

A good question asked in the right way at the right time can cultivate better understanding or awareness of need. Obviously that means questions should be used in a casual manner, not like an interrogation. Ask questions that invite opinions and stimulate thinking. Simple yes or no questions may do the opposite. Good questions should be probing and thought-provoking. For instance, go back to John's problem at the beginning of this chapter. What if he had tried this approach and helped people see their need for small group participation?

He might have begun a conversation with a couple who are new in the church by asking, "What kind of relationships have you made with people in the church?" Or to younger Christians he could have said, "Since you have become a Christian, have you found people to help you find answers to your questions? Has anyone helped you learn to study the Bible?" With people who had been in the church a long time he could have asked them if they had considered the potential of investing spiritually in others.

Questions are probably the simplest way to awaken thirst in people, but there are a few other methods that can be used as well. *Personal testimonies* are often effective in helping people recognize desires and needs in their own life. As they hear of God's working in another person like themselves, they often are stimulated to desire the same thing. *Life experiences* form a laboratory that pinpoints and awakens desires for further growth. The wise leader who is in contact with his people can use those experiences as teachable moments. Or—taking personal experience one step further—you might take another person with you to intentionally create an experience that will open his eyes to the need for growth in his life (e.g., as you share your faith or participate in cross-cultural ministry).

2. PROVIDE INFORMATION ABOUT WHAT MIGHT QUENCH THAT THIRST

Notice that this is the second step, not the first! When there is no felt need, we merely inoculate people against rich opportunities. On the other hand, if some level of thirst has been created, people will be eager for information on how their thirst might be satisfied. This is the time to tell someone about a specific ministry opportunity, a tool he or she should take advantage of, or—in the case of evangelism—the good news of the gospel.

Explain the details a person needs to know in order to be able to make a solid decision. For example, if John had worked to create thirst for the kind of growth that a small group Bible study can cause, his people would have been ready for the details. Without a thirst for small groups all his people heard was another option on the spiritual-activity list.

Providing complete information is also a means of demonstrating your respect for people's ability to make wise decisions. We are not in the business of asking for blind obedience. And we want to avoid pressuring people to make decisions and commitments on the basis of guilt. By providing them with the information they need, we give them room to make decisions at their own speed. We also give the Holy Spirit time and tools to lead people where He would have them go.

A word of caution—before pouring out information, give the salt a chance to make people thirsty. They need time to think. In fact, the larger the commitment you are challenging them to make, the greater the length of time they should be given to make it. Waiting can be very tough, but leaders are looking out for a person's best interest. You know that they could make great strides for Christ if they would do what you are challenging them to do. But you must give them the time and the latitude to make their own decisions at their own speed. To pressure someone is to rob him of the freedom to make his own choice and therefore to dilute his enthusiasm for making a commitment.

3. EXPLAIN THE COST

If there is an area where Christian leaders fall down, it is that we consistently avoid explaining the full cost to our people. We get out the big brush and gloss over specific items. We seem to be afraid that people will say no if they are told everything. Yet to withhold details about the cost of commitment is to commit two major errors. First of all, it is plainly deceitful and will undermine confidence in your leadership. Second, when we withhold the true cost, we are refusing to trust God to do the real convincing. It is dangerous to take His work onto our own shoulders!

This cost may come in any number of forms. When a person makes a step of greater commitment to Christ or to His ministry, there may be a cost in terms of time, energy, vulnerability, money, and so on. Do not be afraid of explaining the true cost. It will not disappear because you fail to mention it. In fact, you will short-circuit a person's commitment if you let him or her make a decision with less than a full understanding of the price.

4. CALL FOR SPECIFIC RESPONSE

At the heart of the challenging process is the desire to help individuals pursue a greater level of involvement or commitment. That is to say a response of some kind is definitely desired. Carefully think through the response that you desire *beforehand.* When you begin to speak with them, make your challenge specific. A general challenge can easily frustrate people because they are not sure how to respond.

If you are challenging someone to take another step of growth, know the specific steps you want him to consider taking. Maybe you will want to provide a specific opportunity to participate in a small group Bible study. Or give them the chance to be part of a six-week class. Specifically challenge them to whatever response is most appropriate—Bible memory, service in ministry, involvement in evangelism, and so on. Clearly identify in your own mind the desired response, and then very specifically challenge them to it.

This opportunity for response should be provided without guilt. We have already talked about avoiding the guilt-trip approach, but this is a good time for a reminder. In our zeal to help people grow in Christ it is tempting to turn the screws a little. However, whenever we use guilt in our attempts to motivate, we place people on a performance acceptance treadmill. Avoid overstating your challenge with guilt-laden phrases such as, "If you care at all about your relationship with Christ, you will . . . " or, "Anyone who has a heart for the lost will . . . "

Also, be cautious about turning your challenge into a situation upon which your own well-being rests. For instance, you do not want to say, "This means so much to me, I hope you won't let me down." Following Christ is the issue, not whether you are disappointed or not. Challenge people to follow Christ and pursue Him, but let Him do the convincing.

APPLIED EXAMPLES OF CHALLENGING PEOPLE

Challenging as a means of encouraging spiritual growth applies to every stage of need. Additionally, this approach will work for the presentation of any ministry opportunity in any context. Whether you are preparing a written flyer or contemplating a one-on-one meeting, these four elements of a challenge provide an excellent approach. Challenging is effective as a ministry tool for people at every stage of spiritual maturity and interest.

NON-CHRISTIANS

With non-Christians we need to relearn the art of creating thirst before we unload the gospel dump truck. Often we unload the gospel message on non-Christians whether they are ready for the whole load or not. A much better approach would be to challenge them with enough good news to satisfy their thirst, then continue attempting to create more thirst.

Jesus had an incredible way of meeting people where they were. He used questions, parables, and real-life situations to create interest. His encounter with the Samaritan woman was initiated when He shattered her predispositions with a simple request for water. Zaccheus's leathery heart was cut wide open when Jesus asked to be his guest. Creating a sense of desire and an awareness of need must precede a presentation of the gospel, or the message will likely fall on deaf ears.

GROWING CHRISTIANS

Growing Christians also benefit from challenging. Regardless of the fact that we would like every Christian to be growing aggressively in Christ, the truth is they are not. Some have plateaued. Others have remained spiritual babes. Still others have grown in their relationship with Christ but not in their service for Christ. Carefully planned challenges will help people recognize the need they have and ways to pursue renewed efforts to grow. It is possible that the reason people have plateaued spiritually is specifically because they were never challenged effectively to take the next steps in their relationship with Christ.

In the equipping process effective challenges can also make a tremendous impact. Because the goal is to enhance the growth of individuals and to multiply the team equipped for ministry, good challenges are ideal tools. What better means is there to help people move to a greater level of ministry training than a well-thought-out challenge? Often we present opportunities heavily wrapped in shoulds and ought-tos. The opportunity to participate in ministry is often presented based upon an idealistic loyalty or sense of intrinsic responsibility, without real thought about the way it fits into the lives of those who might get involved.

Is it possible that appeals frequently go unheeded because they haven't connected with a sense of thirst? Participation in the work of ministry carries a great deal of blessing and enrichment. Our spiritual health and vitality is related to our involvement with others. Why not target these benefits, both individually and corporately, when challenging people to move into greater levels of ministry?

People are hungry for a greater sense of purpose and progress in their lives. Rather than dumping out information about needs in the Body, it might prove more effective to craft specific challenges that connect with people where they are. Each of the seven levels of ministry discussed in chapter 11 offers something deeper and richer. A well planned challenge might often be just the ticket to help a person take another step of ministry training and involvement.

One final thought about this challenging process. Whenever you are challenging someone to a place of service or leadership, it is crucial that you challenge him or her to the vision, not a program. Frequently, people plug into a program as if the goal were merely to keep it going. This approach causes numerous problems. First, when needs shift and it is necessary to alter your program structure, those who felt called to a program find the change threatening. Second, sooner or later the program-focused person will lose perspective on how his involvement contributes to or relates to the whole ministry. Finally, when the hard days come—and they do for every ministry—allegiance to a program is not enough to inspire personal sacrifice. A much better approach is to challenge people to the overall vision for the ministry. When a person feels called to the vision he will view his role as a means of fulfilling it.

Note

1. Dave Busby, "Creating a Willingness Within Students for Spiritual Maturity," in *Discipling the Young Person*, Paul Fleischmann, ed. (San Bernardino, Calif.: Here's Life, 1985), p. 163.

19

POWER TO MAKE IT HAPPEN

Ever played golf? A good day on the course can be beautiful and enjoyable, even great fun. But on a bad day, it can be one of the most humbling experiences you ever willfully inflict upon yourself. There you are, a capable adult staring down at a tiny white ball. In your hand you hold a fairly simple instrument designed to propel that stubborn white ball toward a certain hole merely a few hundred yards down the fairway. If you think about it, there is not much to do really. Swing the club, hit the ball, watch the ball.

On television every weekend, the pros can be seen performing this simple feat, as if it were effortless. Yet most of us who play the game struggle and strain to keep the ball from landing in an area where it cannot be found again. As frustration takes over we try harder. Muscles tighten. Blood pressure rises. Conversation becomes cryptic. The old slice sets new records for distance—sideways. Worms take cover, sand flies, water splashes, and sweat pours. How can a game that is so simple be so difficult?

Certainly many technical flaws may need to be worked out in correcting a faulty golf game. But still, at the heart of it all there are just a few simple principles to integrate in order for things to happen correctly. Above all you need to relax, swing naturally, and let your club do the work it was designed to do.

Is it possible that ministry might be similar? Throughout this book we have examined the principles of ministry as demonstrated by Christ. Not a single one of them is difficult. None of them is hard to understand. All of them have room for growth and development, but none is beyond our reach. Our challenge is to put them into perspective and keep them in balance. Jesus demonstrated this perfect balance. He showed us how each of these important principles of ministry work together and complement one another.

The task of ministry is not intensely complex nor so professionally technical that only "experts" need bother. Serving in the ministry of Christ is a matter of following the basic principles He demonstrated, and resting in His power to change lives. The four phases of His ministry provide a permanent guideline for our own.

1. Build an environment for growth
2. Train a team for ministry
3. Mobilize for evangelism
4. Multiply your leadership base

As in golf, the principles are fairly simple. What's difficult is keeping them in balance and in focus. How will you keep your head on straight? More important, where will the power in your ministry come from? Real power for ministry—as well as living the Christian life—comes through Christ alone.

THE SONLIFE PRINCIPLE

As in every principle of ministry, things must begin in the life of the leader. The Sonlife principle is just such a leader-first principle. Hopefully you will find it to be a source of personal encouragement.

Paul testifies more than 170 times in the New Testament to that which transformed his life. It was "Christ in [me], the hope of glory" (Col. 1:27). Countless other Christians have borne witness to the fact that the reality of "Christ in me" has transformed their lives and ministries as well. Call it the "Christ-life," the "Spirit-filled life," anything you like—the principle is the same. Christ wants to live His life through us. Hence, the "Son-life." This Sonlife principle can be outlined in three simple sentences.

1. THE CHRISTIAN LIFE IS INTENDED TO BE SIMPLE

Paul said it well when he wrote, "I am afraid, lest as the serpent deceived Eve by his craftiness, your minds should be led astray from the simplicity and purity of devotion to Christ" (2 Cor. 11:3, NASB). We face the very real temptation of transforming devotion to Christ and ministry for Christ into a complex, difficult task. This danger is not only internal, it is a target of spiritual warfare.

God's intention was that following Christ and living in devotion to Him be simple and straightforward. Our walk with Christ should be as simple as our belief in Him. "As you therefore have received Christ Jesus the Lord, so walk in Him" (Col. 2:6, NASB). The gospel that brings salvation is good news. That good news is not designed to turn sour after the moment of new birth.

All too often, our propensity to make everything complex invades the realm of our faith and clouds the beauty of God's gift of new life in Christ. If one is to be a "spiritual" Christian we often sound as if there are a multitude of things he or she must do. Follow these rules! Read these books! Go to Bible college or seminary! Learn Greek! Make sure your Bible has gold edges, red letters, and plenty of personal markings to show where you have been reading!

God's intent is that the Christian life be simple. It is to be characterized by the purity of devotion to our Savior. There is one catch. Although simple, the Christian life is not easy.

2. THE CHRISTIAN LIFE IS IMPOSSIBLE

"Impossible" may sound like an overstatement, especially after all of these preceding comments about the simplicity God intends, but the Christian life *is* impossible. Jack Taylor in his book *The Key to Triumphant Living* puts it in perspective with these words:

> Once a person becomes a Christian he is faced with one monstrous dilemma. He is supposed to live, love, walk and talk like Christ. He is commanded to love his enemies, abstain from the very appearance of evil, and grow in grace. Thus we are to worry about nothing and be thankful for everything. We are ordered to rejoice always, deny ourselves, accept the fact of our death, and follow Christ every day of our lives. We are to set our affections on things above and not on things on the earth. Added to these and dozens of other demands made on us, we are supposed to be of good comfort, cheerful, and kind in the midst of an unkind world. This is our dilemma. Paul reflected it when he said, "When I would do good, evil is present with me," (Romans 7:21). He had already said, "I have a desire but how to perform I find not" (Romans 8:18).[1]

The point is that we cannot live the Christian life if we attempt to do so in the power of our own flesh. Jesus said, "Apart from me you can do *nothing*" (John 15:5*b*, italics added). God never intended that we live the Christian life on our own power. Even Jesus Himself did not try to live or minister on His own steam. "The Son can do nothing by himself" (John 5:19). "I can do nothing on My own initiative" (John 5:30, NASB). "It is the Father, living in me, who is doing his work" (John 14:10).

Unfortunately, most of us seem to underestimate the weakness of our flesh and our desperate daily need for the Savior. In ministry that gets very scary. Our tendency is to think, *I am doing OK . . . really I am.* We don't like to admit our powerlessness apart from Christ, so we attempt to do by the flesh what can only be done by the Spirit. Our slogan becomes, "I can do it. At least, I think I can, I think I can, I think I can."

Often our actions would indicate that we believe our need is to study the Bible more, go to church more, give more, serve more, and on and on it goes. But hear the words of Christ, "Apart from me you can do nothing!"

3. THE CHRISTIAN LIFE IS ALLOWING CHRIST TO LIVE HIS LIFE THROUGH US

Only after we come to grips with our complete dependency on Christ can we appreciate the fact that the simple key to the Christian life is Christ's living His life through us. This is the Sonlife principle. Unless we taste and see our need for Him, this principle is little more than words. Let's return to the insights of Jack Taylor.

> There is a simple secret to the Christian life. It is, in fact, so simple that millions miss it. There is a dynamic so mighty that no life can remain the same after discovering it. Paul called it a "mystery which hath been hid from ages and from generations, but now is manifest to his saints" (Col. 1:26). It is THE SECRET, THE KEY, THE SUPREME DYNAMIC, THE GLORIOUS SECRET of the Christian life. I bless the day I began to see it! True Christianity is simply, "Christ-in-you-ity" and "Christ-in-me-ity."[2]

On the one hand the implications of this principle for the work of the ministry are encouraging, but on the other hand they are sobering. To think that God is willing to rescue us from the pit is a wonder of grace. But that He would also be willing to personally carry out the eternal work of His kingdom through us is almost stunning. It is sobering to consider how easily we lose sight of our need for the daily work of Christ and instead attempt ministry in the flesh.

Again we turn to Paul and his inspired insights into the ways the Son lives and works through us—even in spite of us. "'My grace is sufficient for you, for my power is made perfect in weakness.' Therefore I will boast all the more gladly about

my weaknesses, so that Christ's power may rest on me. . . .
For when I am weak, then I am strong" (2 Cor. 12:9-10).

One other significant question remains. This is the question of practicality. If the Christian life is Christ living His life through us and if ministry is accomplished by Christ working through us, then how can we experience this reality? Three basic steps stand out.

1. Know

Perhaps the word *know* is too passive. You really must be convinced of the fact that the Christian life is impossible. Unless you know that apart from Christ you cannot live or serve the way God intends, you'll never get off the starting block. Ultimately, sin is the act or attitude of the person who wants to live independently of God. Faith is the life of dependence upon Him in all our ways. You take the first step when you come to grips with the reality of your absolute dependence upon Christ.

2. Yield

When we recognize our need for Christ to live through us and we want Him to do just that, we are in position to yield to Him. To yield to Christ means to make ourselves available to Him. We give Him the right and the opportunity to set or alter our agenda. We look to Him for wisdom and direction at every turn. We give Him the ownership of all our abilities, energies, and time.

Although this step may sound too unassertive for type A personalities, it is a powerful one. When we yield ourselves to Christ we are opening ourselves up to any work, any activity, any relationship, any decision, anything at all that He might want to do, whenever He might want to do it. And because His agenda and the work of His ministry is what matters most, our absolute availability is the greatest gift we can give Him.

A simple analogy is a water faucet. A faucet's only function is to be available whenever you want to use it. It cannot turn itself on or off. The best faucets are those that offer no resistance and are unclogged so that water might flow freely. Christ wants us to be yielded to His control so that He might freely flow through us at any moment.

3. RESPOND

To respond is to do whatever Christ desires of you. Respond by doing and by depending. As you yield yourself to His control, respond to His direction by doing what He asks in an attitude of dependence upon Him. This step is saying, "OK, Lord, here I am; send me."

Notice that responding comes after yielding. The order is very important. God uses our availability more than any capability, and thus the glory remains His. However, when we offer our capability apart from a yielded spirit, the glory and honor due the Lord can be easily deflected. Furthermore, when we start doing before yielding, we will experience frustration and even legalism. Christ lives through us as we acknowledge our need of Him, yield ourselves to Him, and respond to His leading. It is God's simple plan. It is God's perfect plan.

God has poured out His grace upon you. He is pleased to consider you a "fellow worker" with Himself (1 Cor. 3:9). Therefore set the pace in your ministry by allowing the Lord to begin His work within your own life. Learn to live in daily dependence on Christ as you seek to build a disciple-making ministry. As you follow the principles of Jesus' own ministry you will see the heart of the Great Commission come to life in your midst.

Notes

1. Jack Taylor, *The Key to Triumphant Living* (Nashville: Broadman, 1971), p. 42.
2. Ibid., p. 41.

STUDY GUIDE

By David J. Garda

To grow a healthy church, we must leave theory, theology, and biblical principles and move toward action. This study guide helps you do that through two sections that appear throughout the guide: *Taking Ownership* and *Taking Action*. Our intent is for you to evaluate your ministry in the church and, where necessary, modify or change it totally. The goal is a vibrant, thriving church sensitive to the distinct needs of every attender.

CHAPTER 1

Our Divine Purpose and Passion

Taking Ownership

1. The great commandment that drives the Great Commission is "make disciples." As we note on page 15, "His words hit home loud and clear. In His message was a sincere profound command, 'make disciples.' You knew what He meant because you were a disciple. . . . His plan was that you would help others follow Him just as you had followed Him. Jesus had summarized His passion and His design for ministry that you were to continue. It was identical to the passion for His own ministry."

1. What is your understanding of Christ's command to make disciples?

_____

_____

_____

2. Personally, which relationships and experiences have impacted you to be a disciple? List the persons, by name or position, who have influenced you and what events were involved.

_____

_____

_____

3. Read again the following two sections from chapter 1:

The Great Commission, contrary to many people's thinking, is not just a missions emphasis, nor is it just a focus upon evangelism. It is the mandate of making disciples—a balance of winning people to Christ, building them in their faith, and then equipping them to share in the further work of the Great Commission. *The Great Commission is the primary work of the church!* (p. 17)

We are called to restore to the local church a passion for obeying the Great Commission. (p. 16)

Consider the above two statements. How will your ministry change if disciple making becomes your primary objective rather than merely a program within your ministry?

_____

_____

_____

4. What struggles do you have with establishing the Great Commission as the priority for the church? What struggles would your ministry face in establishing the Great Commission as the priority for the church?

_____

_____

_____

Taking Action

5. How committed is your ministry to Great Commission discipling? Explain:

_____

_____

_____

6. How well do your ministry co-workers share your commitment to Great Commission discipling? How could you measure their commitment better?

_____

_____

_____

7. How accurately do the people who share the leadership in your church understand a Great Commission purpose?

_____

_____

8. What might be done in the near future to communicate God's purpose for the church with the people of the church?

_____

_____

_____

CHAPTER 2
Our Desired Product

Taking Ownership

1. In your own words, why does the local church exist? (What is the purpose of your church?)

_____

_____

_____

_____

_____

2. What does a ministry with a passion to carry out the Great Commission look like? What priorities are essential?

_____

_____

_____

_____

_____

3. What is a Christ-like disciple like? List his or her qualities in the areas of skills, relationships, knowledge, and attitudes.

SKILLS
RELATIONSHIPS
KNOWLEDGE
ATTITUDES

4. What ministry in your church is currently producing disciples with a winning, building, and equipping balance? How could these priorities be expanded into other segments of your church?

_____

_____

_____

Taking Action

1. Please identify the following levels of spiritual interest. In the left column, explain what each individual looks like. In the right, explain your ministry strategy to impact each individual at his level of spiritual interest.

What is this individual like?	How can our church impact this type of individual?
Secular	Winning/Outreach Cultivate
Fringe Attender	Winning/Outreach Sow
Curious	Winning/Outreach Reap
Growing Believer	Building/Growth
Serving Believer	Equipping/Ministry Training
Leader/Shepherd	Leadership Multiplication

2. One principle that must guide our programs is a narrowed focus: "Doing few things well is more effective than doing many things in mediocrity" (p. 30).

Consider that statement. What would change if this were true within your ministry? (If it is already true, how has this practice of specialization affected your area of ministry?)

_____

_____

_____

CHAPTER 3
Christ Our Example

Taking Ownership

1. Reflect upon Christ's ministry. List those insights that you glean for your ministry.

_____

_____

2. A critical foundational element for every ministry is a proper understanding of who Christ is. Draw from your experiences to list six descriptive statements about Jesus. Those statements should have affected your life; explain how those truths have influenced your life.

Who Christ Is	How This Truth Impacts Me

In this chapter we consider the four phases of Jesus' ministry on earth. Phase 1 is foundational. "It was a time in which He devoted Himself to building a foundation that would nurture and sustain significant growth" (p. 36).

3. In building a foundation for His ministry:

a. What did Christ emphasize in His teaching?

_____

_____

b. With whom did Christ spend time?

_____

_____

c. How did Christ teach His followers?

_____

_____

The authors present a key caution in the process of building a ministry: "Never be too hasty to move away from building and maintaining a foundation. Beware of the lure of what lies ahead. The important goals and needs before you can consume you and lead you prematurely away from the foundation of your ministry" (p. 38).

4. What are the dangers of building upon a poor foundation? Look at Matthew 7:24–27 as you consider your answer.

_____

_____

Taking Action

During phase 2, when the team is equipped for ministry, Jesus "made it His habit to seek all kinds of people from all kinds of backgrounds. He paid particular attention to those who were responsive to Him. He had seen that responsiveness in those He called to be His disciples. Now He called them not only to follow Him but to receive special training. He promised to help them become 'fishers of men' (Matt. 4:19; Mark 1:17) and in so doing inaugurated what we might call an 'equipping' or 'ministry training' phase of ministry" (p. 38).

5. Who are the men or women under your care that are ready to be equipped?

_____

_____

6. Are you available to train these people as workers and multipliers? If your schedule limits or excludes your availability, what duties or activities need to be diminished (eliminated?) to allow you to make such training a priority?

_____

7. Identify two individuals and a strategy to expand your equipping ministry with them.

_____

_____

In Phase 3 of His ministry, Jesus actively pursued the masses. "His outreach methodology had a twofold purpose. First and foremost, He was working to reach the masses. Jesus was passionately burdened for the lost and sought to reach out to people everywhere He went. His second purpose was to model the process and involve His ministry team in outreach. He wanted His disciples to share His passion, and He wanted to give them the ability to duplicate His ministry. His desire was to help them succeed in the task of evangelism. He knew the result in their lives would be both deep joy as well as lifelong conviction and commitment to Great Commission living" (p. 40).

8. Read Mark 1:14–2:12. List two insights you gain from observing Christ's outreach priority.

(1) _____

(2) _____

The authors call on ministry leaders to be like Christ by going beyond evangelism talk to "creating avenues of group success. This aspect of our Savior's strategy should be reflected in the corporate strategy of every ministry and every church. . . . It is time to learn how to get involved together in bringing that message to the masses of our generation" (p. 41).

9. How is your ministry assisting believers to be successful in evangelism with their friends?

_____

_____

_____

10. Jesus was often called "a friend of sinners." What sinners would genuinely call you a friend? If no names come to mind, how will you prioritize a friendship with two lost individuals?

(1) _____

(2) _____

How could your ministry help you to reach these "lost" friends?

_____

_____

In phase 4 we restructure for multiplication: "The twelve
. . . had been involved with Him in ministry training and outreach, and now they were ready for shepherding responsibilities" (p. 41; see Matt. 10:1; Mark 3:13–19; Luke 6:12–19).

11. What individuals or influences (teaching, showing,
sending, or involving) have significantly contributed to your
ability to "lead others"?

_____

_____

_____

_____

Tying It Together

As we review the ministry of Christ we often overlook the
everyday nature of those who followed and ministered with
Him. We see three types of believers: they could be called
new, regular, and *super.* But this brand of thinking misses the
point of Jesus life and commission—it's dangerous thinking! We
must affirm that *we* are the people about whom Christ talks. If I
am not qualified to be a disciple, and if I never hope to be a
disciple, then who will be qualified?

Here is a prayer of thanksgiving and dedication that re-
minds us that we remain lifelong disciples called to follow the
Master. Pray the following as a reminder of His call and your
willingness to follow Him:

> Dear Lord, thank you for modeling a life of winning, building,
> and equipping priorities for me. I can't believe that your strat-
> egy to change the world includes me—but I praise you because
> it does! Please help me to be the disciple you invite me to be.
> In Jesus name, _____ (Your Name).

CHAPTER 4
An Environment for Growth

Taking Ownership

We must remember that is God, not us, who brings spiritual growth. "Leadership cannot make growth happen; it is God who causes growth (1 Cor. 3:6). Much as the right climate enables grapes to grow into perfection, the church needs to create an environment that will help people grow" (p. 48).

1. Write a brief prayer of thanksgiving to express your praise to God for the growth He brings.

_____

_____

_____

_____

_____

Taking Action

2. Evaluate how effectively the following priorities are functioning in your ministry by completing the right column.

Foundational Priority	How Are We Doing in this Area?
1. An Atmosphere of Love	1. _____
2. Relational Ministry	2. _____
3. Communicating Christ Clearly	3. _____
4. A Healthy Group Image	4. _____
5. A Prayer Base	5. _____
6. Communicating the Word	6. _____

3. Identify the area of most pressing concern: _____.
Brainstorm ways this need can be addressed during the next
three months.

_____

_____

_____

_____

4. What benefits come by investing your time and resources in a healthy foundation within your ministry?

_____

_____

_____

5. Identify two foundational priorities that you find particularly sensitive to the tyranny of the urgent. What steps are
you willing to take to prevent the urgent from overtaking each
of these top priorities?

Priority a: _____

_____

_____

_____

Priority b: _____

_____

_____

_____

CHAPTER 5
An Atmosphere of Love

Taking Ownership

An atmosphere of love should pervade our interactions because that is Christ's command for his disciples: "A new command I give you: love one another. As I have loved you, so you must love one another. By this all men will know that you are my disciples, if you love one another" (John 13:34–35).

1. What are the practical implications of this passage?

_____

_____

_____

_____

2. According to John's gospel, what are the marks of a true disciple?

a. John 8:31–32 _____

b. John 13:34–35 _____

c. John 15:8 _____

3. The love of a disciple of Christ is in stark contrast to the ways of the world. Give two examples of how your ministry is known for its atmosphere of love.

(1) _____

(2) _____

4. "The task of leaders is to do all we can to create a place where love is genuinely expressed" (p. 58). How have you seen this modeled by other leaders?

_____

_____

_____

Taking Action

5. Below is a chart to help you measure your "love quotient." Put a check mark under the column that best reflects the frequency you practice these loving actions.

Opportunities to Lead in Love	High	Medium	Low
1. Attitude check: Do I really love those under my care?			
2. Do I teach with a tone of love (vs. law)?			
3. Am I a good listener?			
4. Do I model God's love in disappointments?			
5. Do I create situations where love can be expressed?			
6. Do I regularly pray for those under my care?			

6. Read Hebrews 10:24. List at least two acts of love you could demonstrate to "spur on" those under your spiritual care. Then seek opportunities to put that act into practice.

To my spouse _____

_____

_____

To my children _____

_____

_____

Among my ministry team _____

_____

_____

Among those to whom I minister _____

_____

_____

CHAPTER 6
Relational Ministry

Taking Ownership

1. Describe the type of relationship that has helped you grow spiritually (John 3:22).

_____

_____

_____

_____

2. "The point is that the ministry of Jesus was a relational ministry" (p. 70). In what ways do you agree or disagree with this statement?

_____

_____

_____

_____

Taking Action

3. How does a relational priority enable us to fulfill our purpose of "assisting believers to fulfill the Great Commission"?

    a. In the priority of *winning* others to Christ?

_____

_____

_____

    b. In the priority of *building up* believers in Christ?

_____

_____

_____

    c. In the priority of *equipping* believers in Christ?

_____

_____

_____

4. Time is never the problem; the *management* of our time is. Within the context of honest discovery, take five minutes to fill in your realistic weekly schedule, using the grid below. The following codes will help you mark your schedule clearly (Note: more than one code may apply to a single time slot):

TWS: Time with Spouse
TWK: Time with Kids
WORK: Time spent at Work (incl. both home & office based
work.)
DEVO: Planned Time with Christ
MEET: Meetings
R&R: Rest & Relaxation
WIN: Time invested in winning relationships
BUILD: Time invested in building relationships
EQUIP: Time spent in equipping relationships

	SUNDAY	MONDAY	TUESDAY	WEDNESDAY	THURSDAY	FRIDAY	SATURDAY
6 A.M.							
7							
8							
9-10							
11							
NOON							
1-2							
3-4							
5-6							
7							
8							
9							
10							
11-12							

5. Name three changes you can make during the next three months to increase the relational effectiveness of your schedule. How will you accomplish them?

Change #1: _____

_____

Change #2: _____

_____

Change #3: _____

_____

CHAPTER 7
Communicating Christ Clearly

Taking Ownership

1. What misconceptions of Christ have you observed recently?

_____

_____

_____

2. What characteristics of Christ do you cling to:

a. in times of trouble and disappointment? _____

_____

_____

b. in times of joy? _____

_____

_____

c. in times of stress? _____

_____

_____

d. in times of unmet needs? _____

_____

_____

Taking Action

3. Communicating Christ clearly to the world around you is important. How can you communicate a proper concept of Christ to the following:

a. your co-workers? ⎯⎯⎯⎯⎯⎯⎯

⎯⎯⎯⎯⎯⎯⎯⎯⎯⎯⎯⎯⎯⎯⎯⎯

b. your family members? ⎯⎯⎯⎯⎯⎯⎯

⎯⎯⎯⎯⎯⎯⎯⎯⎯⎯⎯⎯⎯⎯⎯⎯

c. a spiritually lost peer, family member, or associate? ⎯

⎯⎯⎯⎯⎯⎯⎯⎯⎯⎯⎯⎯⎯⎯⎯⎯

d. those under your spiritual care? ⎯⎯⎯⎯⎯⎯

⎯⎯⎯⎯⎯⎯⎯⎯⎯⎯⎯⎯⎯⎯⎯⎯

⎯⎯⎯⎯⎯⎯⎯⎯⎯⎯⎯⎯⎯⎯⎯⎯

4. Retell a Scripture event in the first person. Remember, you are one of the characters (an eyewitness) of the event. Help us to feel, smell, hear, and join you in your meeting with the Savior.

⎯⎯⎯⎯⎯⎯⎯⎯⎯⎯⎯⎯⎯⎯⎯⎯

⎯⎯⎯⎯⎯⎯⎯⎯⎯⎯⎯⎯⎯⎯⎯⎯

⎯⎯⎯⎯⎯⎯⎯⎯⎯⎯⎯⎯⎯⎯⎯⎯

⎯⎯⎯⎯⎯⎯⎯⎯⎯⎯⎯⎯⎯⎯⎯⎯

⎯⎯⎯⎯⎯⎯⎯⎯⎯⎯⎯⎯⎯⎯⎯⎯

5. Spend time in prayer celebrating the character, person, and ministry of Jesus in your life.

CHAPTER 8
A Healthy Group Image

Taking Ownership

1. Read Acts 2:43–47. Illustrate the following evidences of a healthy group image from your own experiences with a group in your current (or past) church.

a. They were devoted (v. 42). _____

_____.

_____

b. They were together with oneness (vv. 44, 46). _____

_____

_____

c. There was a sense of gladness (vv. 46–47). _____

_____

_____

d. They enjoyed the favor of all the people (v. 47). _____

_____

_____

2. Seeing problems over potential is contagious. Do you remember the ten spies who saw the problems as Joshua and Caleb saw the potential? Do you remember the big Goliath in the eyes of Israel, but the bigger God in the eyes of young David? In what way does our concept of Christ affect our willingness to view our ministries with "potential-filled" versus "problem-finding" eyes?

_____

_____

_____

Taking Action

3. What testimonies of God's working need to be told to those within your ministry? List the names of five people who need to proclaim how Christ has shown Himself to be powerful and present.

a. _____

b. _____

c. _____

d. _____

e. _____

4. What is a creative or fresh way to communicate these testimonies within your ministry?

_____

_____

5. Identify a regular way to communicate these stories to those within your ministry.

_____

_____

More than anything else, Christianity is relationships. Consider the close relationships described in the early church:

They were devoted. (Acts 2:42)
They were together with oneness. (vv. 44, 46)
There was a sense of gladness. (vv. 46–47)
They enjoyed the favor of all the people. (v. 47)

6. As followers of Christ, we have many relationships too. First and foremost is a relationship with our heavenly Father. How can you help those under your spiritual care to become devoted to the Great Commission purpose that God has given His church?

_____

_____

7. Also important is a relationship with our brothers and sisters in Christ. What will you do to contribute to a healthy (oneness, gladness, favor) group image among those with whom you minister?

_____

_____

CHAPTER 9
A Prayer Base

Taking Ownership

"The kingdom of God does not consist in words, but in power" (1 Cor. 4:20, NASB). Neither is it defined by "programs, curriculum, video libraries, creative clip-art, or any other ministry tool" (p. 100). That is why prayer is paramount for the church leader.

1. Read Mark 1:35; Matthew 14:23-25; and Luke 6:12-13. What three conclusions can you draw from these texts?

Conclusion #1: _____

_____

Conclusion #2: _____

_____

Conclusion #3: _____

_____

Taking Action

2. Flip back a few pages and compare these conclusions with your schedule from chapter 6. What one surgical adjustment could be made to bring your schedule into more conformity with your conclusions?

_____

_____

_____

"Prayer is one of the most important aspects of building disciples. If we are to help people grow in their knowledge of Jesus Christ we must pray. In fact, if we do everything else right, but fail to pray, nothing significant will happen" (Carl Wilson, *With Christ in the School of Discipleship*).

3. What is one adjustment to your ministry agenda, events, or schedule that can help you to simply implement Christ prayer priority within your ministry?

_____

_____

_____

4. Read Exodus 33:15. Spend time in prayer—making this prayer of Moses your personal plea.

CHAPTER 10
Communicating the Word

Taking Ownership

1. What "funny" misconceptions of Bible stories or Christian living can you remember from your childhood or the childhood of others?

_____

_____

_____

2. As adults these misconceptions become dangerously wrong road maps for living. How have you witnessed a wrong biblical concept, or a wrong concept of God, sidetrack a life?

_____

_____

_____

3. "Always keep your finger in the text" (p. 109). Why do you think we so easily shift from this insight?

_____

_____

_____

4. What suggestions could you offer to help a study group "keep their fingers in the text?"

_____

_____

_____

"Communicating the Word is so fundamental to ministry that none of us will ever outlive our need to increase our effectiveness" (p. 116).

Taking Action

5. The six priorities presented in chapters 5–10 summarize the essentials for growing a healthy believer. Complete and discuss the "Evaluating Your Environment of Growth" work sheets found on pages 117–20.

CHAPTER 11
The Nature of Ministry Training

Taking Ownership

"Follow Me, . . . and I will make you fishers of men" (Matt. 4:19). A crucial part of Jesus' ministry vision was to equip His disciples to do the work that He commissioned them to do after His ascension. We also are to equip others to do the work of the kingdom.

1. Write a practical definition of "equipping":

_____

_____

_____

2. Share an experience you have had that illustrates this practical definition (draw from any context, i.e., schooling, career, sports, hobbies, ministry):

_____

_____

_____

3. Why is an equipping process (i.e., M^1–M^7) so critical?

_____

_____

_____

_____

4. In your own words, explain why Great Commission equipping must include a balance of Peer Care (a people intensive ministry in the life of believers, M^4) and Peer Evangelism (a people intensive ministry in the life of unbelievers, M^5–M^7).

_____

_____

_____

_____

Taking Action

5. Brainstorm the skills necessary to accomplish the twofold agenda of Ministry Training—peer care, and peer evangelism.

Skills Needed for Peer Care	Skills Needed for Peer Evangelism

6. In the above chart, place an asterisk next to the two most critical skills for your current ministry in each column.

a. Identify two individuals who may have the desire to learn and apply these four skills.

1. _____ 2. _____

b. What will be your strategy to equip them in these skills?

_____

_____

_____

_____

_____

CHAPTER 12

Identifying the Responsive

Taking Ownership

1. Looking back on our study in chapter 11, what qualities or factors led you to select the two individuals in question 6?

_____

_____

_____

2. What qualities or factors, do you think, led Christ to select certain individuals to be equipped?

_____

_____

_____

3. What questions could you ask to measure your growth in each of the following areas?

Faithful: As measured by _____

_____

Available: As measured by _____

_____

Teachable: As measured by _____

_____

Enthusiastic: As measured by _____

_____

Taking Action

"Ask the Lord of the Harvest, therefore, to send out workers into his harvest field" (Matt. 9:38).

4. Take a moment and pray specifically for God to fulfill Matthew 9:38 within your ministry.

5. Identify your most effective skill in ministry: _____

_____

_____

How could you train two individuals to excel beyond your own abilities in this area?

_____

_____

_____

_____

CHAPTER 13
Training the Team

Taking Ownership

1. In what ways have you seen evidence of *imparting your life* to another? (1 Thess. 2:8; Luke 6:40).

_____

_____

2. List the small and large insights, skills, priorities, knowledge, and relationships that have been critical to your growth and ministry in Christ:

Insights	Skills	Priorities	Knowledge	Relationships

3. From the above list, place an asterisk next to the top two lessons in each area. Which lessons have produced the greatest fruit from your ministry?

_____

_____

_____

_____

Taking Action

"One of the common mistakes of the equipping process is that it lacks an intentional approach" (p. 141).

4. The guidelines of ministry training are: *impart your life, challenge people to involvement, support your team with training,* and *keep your focus clear.* Which of these areas reflects an equipping strength in your current ministry?

_____

_____

Which of these areas reflects an equipping weakness in your current ministry?

_____

_____

Within your ministry, who is uniquely gifted to assist your ministry to strengthen your equipping process?

_____

5. Reflect back to the manual transmission illustration on page 144. List three field trips or field experiences that are necessary for your workers to become Great Commission effective? (This includes a balance of winning, building, and equipping priorities on a personal and a ministry level.)

a. _____

_____

b. _____

_____

c. _____

_____

6. Identify your ministries (or areas of a specific ministry) that have the greatest need of workers:

a. _____

_____

b. _____

_____

c. _____

_____

Invest your life and energy in a person
*   to make a spiritual difference.*
Focus on imparting your life.
Spiritual preparation is a high priority.
Prioritize people over the task or program.

7. What training strategy can you develop that will increase your effectiveness at producing workers with this Ministry Mind-set vs. the Project Mentality (p. 147).

_____

_____

_____

_____

_____

8. Through prayer, express to God your eagerness or apprehension about building a ministry that meets people at their point of spiritual need and helps them grow as disciples. Express your desire to have Him lead you as the depth and breadth of your discipling ministry increases.

CHAPTER 14
Rethinking Evangelism

Taking Ownership

1. "The majority of [Christians] believe they cannot be successful in sharing their faith" (The Barna Group, p. 151). As you reflect upon this quote, list why you think most believers have bought into the concept that only a few within the body of Christ can effectively be committed to evangelism?

_____

_____

_____

_____

2. Re-read Matthew 28:18–20. How does Christ's strategy counteract this misconception?

_____

_____

_____

_____

3. Why is evangelism difficult to accomplish alone? How does our evangelistic equipping change when we include a commitment to share together in evangelizing our peers?

_____

_____

_____

4. How has a relationship with another believer helped you in an evangelistic relationship?

_____

_____

_____

5. Identify the ways your church has assisted you in reaching a lost friend or peer.

_____

_____

_____

Taking Action

6. Outline a three-event strategy that will model the cultivating, sowing, and reaping process within our evangelistic relationships. The events or activities can be spread over three consecutive months, three consecutive weekends, or even over three consecutive nights.

Outreach Event A: Primary purpose *cultivating*

_____

_____

_____

Outreach Event B: Primary purpose *sowing*

_____

_____

_____

Outreach Event C: Primary purpose *reaping*

_____

_____

_____

CHAPTER 15

Mobilizing for Evangelism

Taking Ownership

1. Jesus was often called a *friend of sinners*. Identify the nonbelievers who would genuinely call you their friend:

_____

_____

_____

2. Select one of the above individuals. How can you affirm this relationship during the next week?

_____

_____

_____

Taking Action

"The Gospel is news to each generation, and we must seek new ways to address our times" (R. C. Sproul). In our increasingly secular culture, the unchurched have a decreasing knowledge about Christ and the Scriptures. Within this context the traditional concept of a one-shot outreach event can actually hinder the process of lifestyle evangelism. It is the Holy Spirit empowered life of an authentic believer with a nonbelieving friend that actually energizes our outreach events. The event becomes a forum to spark a conversation about Christ and His impact, rather than a monolog gospel presentation. As believers share together the responsibilities for these consistent body evangelism events, the more equipped they will become in exposing their peers to Christ.

3. Prepare a strategy for your plan to further the team approach of evangelism within your ministry. How can you specifically counter the misconception that evangelism is primarily a lone ranger responsibility?

_____

_____

_____

_____

4. Read Luke 15, especially noting verse 10. When was the last time you had the first-hand experience of rejoicing in the finding of a lost soul? Spend time in prayer. Commit yourself to the finding of a lost soul in much the same way as Luke 15 presents the search for the lost coin, lost sheep, and a lost life.

CHAPTER 16
Leadership Multiplication

Taking Ownership

1. Read Exodus 18. What leadership principles do you draw from this passage?

_____

_____

_____

2. *Reflect:* Moses became willing to share his leadership responsibility with faithful and capable believers. What do we communicate when we function as a lone ranger leader?

_____

_____

_____

3. *React:* Whereas all believers are ultimately called to an equipping ministry, only a few are called to a leadership ministry. This is especially true when we define the leadership ministry as the role of an elder or shepherd.

_____

_____

_____

4. What insights do the following verses offer on understanding the role and character of leadership?

1 Timothy 3:1 _____

_____

1 Timothy 5:22 _____

_____

Ephesians 4:11–13 _____

_____

James 3:1 _____

_____

2 Timothy 2:2 _____

_____

1 Peter 5:3 _____

_____

Titus 1:5–6 _____

_____

CHAPTER 17
Cultivating Vision

Taking Ownership

1. Write down your vision for your current ministry:

_____

_____

_____

_____

2. How well does the vision of your church reflect the balance of winning, building, and equipping priorities that we draw from the Great Commission?

_____

_____

3. Which aspects of your vision do you especially own as your passion?

_____

_____

Taking Action

4. With a clearly communicated vision we can evaluate fruitfulness in light of effectiveness, rather than mere quantity

or efficiency. We become caught in the trap of doing things right, without being certain that we are doing the right things! Use the following work sheets to sharpen your handle on the unique vision that God has called you to within His Great Commission objective.

THE PAST: How has God worked in my life? What has happened in your life that has shaped the ministry burdens or passions within you? What experiences or relationships have God used to clarify His purpose for your life?

THE PRESENT: What opportunity of ministry causes me to light up? What needs am I, or my church, in a unique position to meet? I find myself especially sensitive to the challenge of _____.

THE FUTURE POTENTIAL: In my wildest dreams, I sense that God wants to do this in _____ ministry over the next _____ (number of) years. Five years from now, what will our ministry look like? If God blessed you with unlimited resources, what would you desire to see most thoroughly accomplished for Christ's cause?

5. Clarify your vision by defining three areas of maximum impact:

A. _____

B. _____

C. _____

6. Update or create a vision statement (either for your ministry or for your life) that draws from the unique ministry of God in your past and present, plus your dreams for the future.

_____

_____

_____

7. How can this vision be remembered and owned by those within your ministry? How will this vision be communicated in a simple, yet memorable, way?

_____

_____

The Act of Challenging

Taking Ownership

At the beginning of chapter 18, we read about the disappointing experience of Pastor John: "By the time registration was finished, only three people had signed up. Three people wouldn't even comprise one healthy group, not to mention the fact that all three apparently signed up because they felt sorry for their pastor. After all, 'This program seemed so important to him'" (p. 198).

1. What lessons have you learned from experiences similar to the above illustration?

_____

_____

_____

2. With all of our best intentions we easily slip into a *Program-Based Design* for ministry rather than a discipling *People-Based Design*. Why do we feel such a pressure to measure success by the size of an event rather than the progress within people's lives?

_____

_____

3. How could Pastor John have changed his approach from promoting a ministry to a more People-Based Design for their involvement?

_____

_____

4. How did Jesus challenge individuals to a deeper ministry involvement?

John 1:39–43 _____

Matthew 9:9 _____

Mark 1:17 _____

Luke 14:27–33 _____

Taking Action

5. Develop a challenge for the following opportunities (see pp. 201-5).

You are inviting a friend to an outreach event:

Create thirst _____

_____

A drink of information _____

_____

The cost (time, energy, funds) _____

_____

How will they specifically respond? _____

_____

You are recruiting a couple to join your small group Bible studies:

Create thirst _____

_____

A drink of information _____

_____

The cost (time, energy, funds) _____

_____

How will they specifically respond? _____

_____

You are challenging a believer to be equipped for a ministry of _____:

Create thirst _____

_____

A drink of information _____

_____

The cost (time, energy, funds) _____

_____

How will they specifically respond? _____

_____

CHAPTER 19
Power to Make it Happen

Taking Ownership

"The task of ministry is not intensively complex nor so professionally technical that only 'experts' need bother. Serving in the ministry of Christ is a matter of following the basic principles He demonstrated, and resting in His power to change lives. The four phases of His ministry provide a permanent guideline for our own" (p. 210).

1. List three insights into the strategy of Christ that you have owned during the course of this study:

a. _____

b. _____

c. _____

2. Read 2 Corinthians 11:3. How have you observed the truths of this verse to be true?

_____

_____

_____

3. Read Colossians 2:6. Why is growth in Christ as supernatural an event as salvation in Christ?

_____

_____

_____

4. Read John 15:5, 15, 30. How do you react to this truth?

_____

_____

_____

Taking Action

5. Read 2 Corinthians 12:9–10. It is an incredible mystery: the Creator of the universe has chosen to work in and through you, and every other believer who is willing yield his life. The concept of new, regular, and super saints needs to get thrown out the window. In its place we must rest in His promise to gift us to be sufficient for our discipling call. Turn to the Father in prayer and yield yourself to His purpose and respond to the single command of the Great Commission—make disciples.

Appendix

For almost fifteen years, Sonlife Ministries has trained church leadership. The material in this book has been drawn in part from the Sonlife Strategy Seminar and the Growing a Healthy Church Seminar. Although Sonlife began with a primary focus on youth ministries, our efforts and commitment now are actively oriented toward the entire local church.

Annually twenty thousand leaders experience some aspect of Sonlife training. The ministry has grown out of the Strategy Seminar into a proven series of training seminars designed to equip local church leadership. Training and support tools are now available for ministry leaders in every segment of your church.

Total church track

The *Growing a Healthy Church I* seminar: a seven-hour overview of the development of a Great Commission healthy church. This seminar gives Jesus' foundations for ministry and applies it to the local church.

The *Growing a Healthy Church II* seminar: a ten-hour guided workshop for implementing a winning, building, and equipping balance in your church. Prerequisite: GHC I.

The *Growing a Healthy Church III* seminar: three days of intensive training in being a leader that equips the saints to share in the work of ministry. Prerequisite: GHC II.

The *Growing a Healthy Church IV* seminar: three days of intensive training in being a leader who multiplies leaders.

Student ministry track

The *Strategy Seminar:* an eight-hour overview of the discipling process. The Strategy is the hub of Sonlife's youth training. This seminar draws from the life of Christ and applies His philosophy for reaching this generation for Jesus Christ. Biblically based and principle oriented, the Strategy Seminar is readily transferable to any ministry setting.

Youth Ministry Foundations: eight hours of team training for youth leaders and ministry-level students. Principles from the Strategy Seminar are joined with resources and tools to launch your team into "Great Commission" ministry. Workshops cover six priorities for student ministry that provide a biblical foundation for life change.

Advanced I: dig deeper into the Strategy principles while being equipped with tools for vision, assessment, team building, and equipping others to minister. Prerequisite: Sonlife Strategy Seminar.

Advanced II: a seminar designed to teach leadership multiplication skills. Learn the skills of consulting and leadership expansion principles within the movement of a discipling ministry. Prerequisite: Advanced I.

Audio Training

The *How To Series:* Bite-sized pieces of the Strategy Seminar are aimed at enhancing group ownership of Great Commission priorities. Each seminar features a separate workbook and four training sessions. Included in the series are: "How to Create a Caring Community," "How to Balance your Programming," "How to Sharpen Your Contacting Skills," "How to Begin Group Outreach," and "How to Begin your Ministry Team." Contact Sonlife Resources at (708) 682-2950 to request a free catalog.

As you seek direction for your ministry, consider Sonlife as a source of help. Sonlife desires each training event or resource to be an encouraging, equipping, and motivating experience for you. The training is biblically based, principle oriented, and team applied. We are excited about your joining the movement of church-centered "Great Commission" ministry.

For more information on seminar locations and the training of Sonlife Ministries, you can write us at:

Sonlife Ministries
1119 Wheaton Oaks Court
Wheaton, IL 60187-3051
(708) 682-2959